Touching accounts of real-life situations are surrounded by life-changing lessons from "God principles" and personal experiences. The author presents from Psalm 139 how everyone is "wonderfully made" but there are temptations that can potentially bind one in chains. *Unshackled* demonstrates how the power of God makes it possible to break free from those chains.

The author skillfully presents practical ways of becoming free, and "If the Son makes you free, you will be free indeed." This theme is woven throughout this wonderful presentation of how to become free. *Unshackled* shows how personal development will be enhanced by establishing a strong relationship with God and others. It was hard to put this book down as I became gripped by the compelling accounts of how so many overcame problems to become Unshackled.

—**Ziden L. Nutt**
Founder and Director
Emeritus of Good News Productions, International

A person does not have to be in jail or in prison to be "locked up." People go to work, go to school, go to church, go to sporting events, and yet they are in prison. They are handcuffed by either something someone has done to them or by the choices they have made. They are locked up and don't know how to get out.

Unshackled is about real life, real people, and real solutions of people who have been in this prison. Peggy Park has hit a home run for the thousands who will read this and apply what the people telling their stories have done to get out of the chains that are around their lives. She gives us hope, a plan, and the message that you can break free and out of the prison that has you shackled. A person cannot go back and make a brand new start, but they can start today and make a brand new ending!

Are you crying out for help and no one hears you? Want to get out of those handcuffs? I highly recommend reading *Unshackled*.

—**Whit Criswell**
Co-Teaching Pastor
Mt. Zion Christian Church, Winchester, Kentucky

In *Unshackled* Peggy Park couples her God-given wisdom and insight with real-life stories of individuals who have experienced the delivering power of our Lord. This is a "must read" in this hour when so many are struggling with fears, addictions, hurts, and issues that need only a touch from the Master in order for their shackles to be loosed! Read in faith and trust God to destroy every yoke and stronghold in your life!

—**Evangelist Leslie Bishop**
Author, Assistant Pastor
The Temple of Healing Waters, Sterling, Virginia

Founder and CEO
of Led by Jesus Ministries and "Women in Ministry Getaways"

UNSHACKLED

UNSHACKLED

• Experiencing True Freedom for Men and Women •

PEGGY PARK

WinePressPublishing
Great Books, Defined.

The above symbol marks the true stories of those who contributed to the book.

ISBN 13: 978-1-60615-176-1
ISBN 10: 1-60615-176-2
Library of Congress Catalog Card Number: 2011924914

Unshackled is dedicated to my husband, George, who has stood by me as I have struggled to become free in Christ. I also dedicate this book to my three children, Susan, Andrew, and Margaret. They witnessed many of my spiritual challenges as I have discovered the peace to be found in embracing God's principles, which lead to true freedom.

CONTENTS

ACKNOWLEDGMENTS

I am grateful to Marion Barna and Chris Henderson for their suggestions and editing. Kathy Mitchell was a great help as she read the manuscript in its very early stages. My husband, George, has applied his editing skills and has been a constant encourager.

Note: For readers who are not familiar with the Christian Bible, please be aware that there are many versions. The version I am quoting in any one place is indicated in the text as follows:

NKJV (New King James Version)
NIV (New International Version)
NLT (New Living Translation)
AMP (Amplified)
MESSAGE (Message)

INTRODUCTION

Do you drag through life ensnared by addictions, old hurts, memories, and disappointments? Do you harbor unforgiveness toward those who have wounded you? Are you living your life depressed, angry, and insecure? Do memories buried deep under the surface cause you to strike out as your pain erupts? How do we get into the messes that shackle us? And how can we get out?

Freedom is possible. That is good news! Freedom awaits all who suffer from the chains that bind us. There is a path out of troubling behavior and thoughts that many experience. In this book are the accounts of numerous individuals who have faced challenging life circumstances and then broken free of the chains that held them captive.

True freedom comes as we discover and accept the person God created us to be. It grows as we follow the teachings our Creator gave to ensure freedom on the part of those who chose to obey those teachings. Often that unique person has been buried under layers of guilt and shame, and has a misconception of God and self. In this book you will read the true accounts of numerous individuals who have faced challenging life circumstances and broken free of the chains that held them captive.

Jennie's mother once told her, "I wish you had never been born." The statement was later retracted, but the bruise was buried deep.

Marge had to face her preacher husband's sexual addiction when she discovered pornographic material stored in the trunk of his car. She got an eye full, including videos of him engaged in sex with other women in hotels, and even in their own home.

Sam was a respected public figure in his small town, but he had a secret gambling addiction. He simply could not stop and was always convinced that the next bet would come up a winner. Eventually he found himself deeply in debt, having mortgaged his home to the limit and embezzled money from the bank where he worked. Suicide seemed the only answer. Fortunately, he could not follow through.

Ralph broke his mother's heart when she found out he had bought a nightclub and topless women were a part of the scene. He was using uppers, downers, and pot, often mixing these with large amounts of alcohol. It is a miracle that he lived to tell his story.

Witness the freedom as the chains of oppression, depression, old memories, addictions, and distorted thinking lose their power. Celebrate as each person relates his or her story of breaking free.

Where Do Chains Originate?

Some chains are the result of things done to us. Some chains are the result of what we needed that we did not have. Although many are due to our own choices, there is hope. The storytellers found it in the teachings of one who suffered more than any of us can imagine. His name was Jesus. Read what the storytellers have to say, and then decide for yourself if the subjects are truly free. Have they been transformed? Did they experience freedom from the chains that had them bound? That is the test of whether this book is worth your consideration.

Together we will explore the reasons we get into the things that challenge and shackle us.

Chapter 1

PATHWAY TO FREEDOM

Journey back with me some six thousand years to a paradise called The Garden of Eden. Scholars are not in agreement as to the exact location. Here we discover how humankind became shackled. Picture a beautiful garden with every imaginable flower, tree, and foliage. Flowing streams of water run through the grounds.

Adam and Eve, the first man and woman, were created to live freely in unbroken fellowship in this paradise with God, their Creator. Adam walked and talked with God. This friendship was broken when an evil force in the form of a serpent subtly interjected doubts into Eve's mind concerning God. The tempter (Satan) appeared to Eve in the form of a snake and enticed her to eat of the one tree in the garden God had declared off-limits.

> Now the serpent was more crafty than any of the wild animals the Lord God had made. He said to the woman, "Did God really say, 'You must not eat from any tree in the garden'?" The woman said to the serpent, "We may eat fruit from the trees in the garden, but God did say, 'You must not eat fruit from the tree that is in the middle of the garden, and you must not touch it, or you will die.'" "You will not surely die," the serpent said to the woman. "For God knows that when you eat of it your eyes will be opened, and you will be like

God, knowing good and evil." When the woman saw that the fruit of the tree was good for food and pleasing to the eye, and also desirable for gaining wisdom, she took some and ate it. She also gave some to her husband, who was with her, and he ate it. Then the eyes of both of them were opened.

—Genesis 3:1–7 NIV

"You will be like God, knowing good and evil," the Devil told Eve. She was snared. Adam listened to Eve's story of what happened between her and the Serpent in the garden, and he also succumbed to the appeal of the fruit. When they chose to follow the sly suggestion and ate the forbidden fruit, they came under the curse of sin and death. This set up a pattern for mankind to think we know better than God.

Chains of oppression, affliction, and curses wrapped around them. They were no longer free. The chains were not visible but were nevertheless very real. Adam and Eve were spiritually separated from God and became self-conscious when they became aware of being naked before their Maker. They lost their innocence. We continue to reap the legacy of their decision, for according to Scripture, "I, the Lord your God, am a jealous God who will not tolerate your affection for any other gods. I lay the sins of the parents upon their children; the entire family is affected—even children in the third and fourth generations of those who reject me" (Exod. 20:5 NLT).

The way for a person to break away from this cycle of sin is to accept Jesus as Lord and Savior and allow him to transform one's life. God's desire was for all of us to remain pure in our fellowship with him. When Satan lured Adam and Eve away from God's plan for them, their sweet, unsullied relationship with God was broken. A barrier sprang up between God and his human creation. We read in the book of Isaiah in the Bible that "your iniquities have separated you from your God; your sins have hidden his face from you, so that he will not hear" (59:2 NIV).

Freedom of Choice

We have the choice to take the pathway that will set us free, or we can continue in our stubborn self-will and govern ourselves by our intuition, impulses, and selfish determination. Sheer willpower may work for a time as we address our individual chains, but true lasting freedom can only be found by following the guidelines of the one who created us. There is a source that provides the power for each of us to shed the chains that bind. As amazing as it sounds, we can have God living in us in the form of the Holy Spirit. With him we can experience true freedom and transformation.

Reconciliation

Although he did know they would choose their own way, God was not behind Adam and Eve's choice to disobey. Even before the original pair fell out of fellowship with God, God had a plan to restore fellowship between him and his creation. The pattern was laid down in the Old Testament that blood sacrifices (animals) were required to give the children of Israel a means for their sins to be forgiven. This was a picture of the death of Christ (referred to as the Lamb of God) whose life would be sacrificed for the sins of the world. Where the Old Testament sacrifices had to be offered on a continual basis, the sacrifice of Jesus was a onetime offering. The book of Leviticus in the Bible states that the life of the body is in its blood: "I have given you the blood on the altar to purify you, making you right with the Lord. It is the blood, given in exchange for a life, that makes purification possible" (17:11 NLT). Jesus willingly went to the cross to provide that blood sacrifice for any man, woman, or child choosing to forsake their sins and be transformed. It is amazing that he provided not only for every sin ever committed, but for every sin not yet committed—even to end of the ages. In a mystery beyond full comprehension, God revealed through his Son his true heart toward his human creation. He gave his blood to provide the sacrifice for our sins.

Power/Provision

The power of God is great enough to break any habit, addiction, or oppression. Fifty-year-old Rodney, who owns a successful heating and air conditioning business, told me an amazing story that demonstrates how a life can be changed. He said, "When I was eighteen years old, I was rejected by my music teacher. I was his right-hand man, directing the choir in his absence and performing other duties. Everybody said I would win the award for the most talented student in my high school. Yet, when the time came, the teacher did not nominate me! It could have been due to the color of my skin. Black people hardly got any attention back then. This was especially painful because I was musically accomplished. The award should have been mine."

Following this heartbreaking rejection, Rodney declared, "'I am quitting music all together, and I will turn to drugs as my answer.' I went into full-blown rebellion against God for three years. I rode around town drunk, used and sold marijuana and cocaine, and was into wild, crazy partying. I was also addicted to cigarettes. Then one day a friend was brave enough to say, 'Rodney, Jesus is the way, the truth, and the life. He is the only way to God, the Father. Getting to heaven is not through a church or through a religion, and it is not through self-righteous behavior. The way is through a real man named Jesus who walked and talked with people whose lives were far from perfect.'

"As I was taking a shower the words came out of my mouth, 'Jesus, I am clean on the outside but my heart is dirty. I ask forgiveness for my sins and ask you to come and live in me.' I felt a power inside of me that I had never had before. I stepped out of the shower, wrapped myself in a towel, got on my knees and asked God to take the desire for drugs from me. For three days I was so sick that I just lay on the bed sweating, trembling violently, hallucinating, and throwing up. I was in my own hell as I went through this. God had told my praying mother that I would be set free after three days. That is exactly what happened. I was totally free from any desire for drugs. I fell in love with Jesus. I praise him for his wonderful blood sacrifice and his power that saved me from an eternity without him. I praise him for providing me freedom from the addiction to drugs, alcohol, and cigarettes. The defeat I felt as a result of my music teacher's lack of support for my God-given musical ability has been removed. I now use my voice to sing for God's glory."

Sin Bearer

Jesus bore the sins of all humanity as he hung on the cross and was forsaken by his heavenly Father. Because God is holy and cannot be related to sin in any degree, Jesus had to be fully separated from the Father as he was made sin for our sins (2 Cor. 5:20 NKJV). Jesus' nailed hands were stretched out to humanity as if to say, "Come to me." His body was beaten, bruised, and pierced. He suffered physical thirst and, more painful still, spiritual thirst as he felt his Father's presence withdrawn from him. He cried, "'*Eli, Eli, lema sabachthani?*' which means 'My God, my God, why have you abandoned me?'" (Matt. 27:46 NLT).

Decision

There is a time in each person's life when they become accountable for making the decision to accept Jesus' payment for their wrongdoing. If the decision is to accept the restored fellowship with God through receiving Jesus' blood sacrifice for their sins, then God's Holy Spirit takes up residency in the person. God's Spirit actually comes and lives in those who invite him to do so. Is this not amazing?

For those who refuse the sacrifice made for them and instead walk in self-will (manifested as active rebellion or passive indifference), Satan becomes their master—whether the person is conscious of it or not. *There is no neutral ground.* If someone does not choose Jesus, then that person has chosen against Jesus.

On the matter of deciding for or against Jesus, some people have told me they have not decided and that they will decide later. Sobering words from Scripture show us that we are deceived if we believe this. "Anyone who isn't with me opposes me, and anyone who isn't working with me is actually working against me" (Matt. 12:30 NLT).

My friend Rodney identified the following steps to transformation and a new life. The steps lead to what the Bible calls the new birth.

Steps to Transformation

❖ Recognize you are a sinner. "For all have sinned; all fall short of God's glorious standard" (Rom. 3:23 NLT).

❖ Be willing to confess and repent of your sins. "… you will also perish unless you turn from your evil ways and turn to God" (Luke 13:3 NLT).

- ❖ Believe Jesus Christ shed his blood for you on the cross and provided forgiveness for your sins. "But God showed His great love for us by sending Christ to die for us while we were still sinners" (Rom. 5:8 NLT).
- ❖ Through prayer, invite Jesus Christ to come into your life and be your Lord and Savior. "But to all who believed him and accepted him, he gave the right to become children of God" (John 1:12 NLT).
- ❖ Follow Jesus' example and be baptized. "Anyone who believes and is baptized will be saved. But anyone who refuses to believe will be condemned" (Mark 16:16 NLT).

Act of the Will

The personal transformation that the Bible calls the new birth is not merely an intellectual belief that Jesus Christ is the Son of God, nor is it simply an emotional experience. It is an act of a person's will to acknowledge their wrongdoing, and, by faith, invite Jesus into his or her life. With the acts of belief, confession, repentance, and baptism we are inviting Jesus to rule and transform our lives. In the new birth, God in the form of spirit (the Holy Spirit) comes into our lives and actually lives inside of us. This means that men and women have the very life and nature of God within. They have been born again—born of the Spirit of God. What an incredible thought! It is truly beyond comprehension. This is not the same as the statement made by many in the public eye today who say, "I am god, and you are god. God is everywhere and in each of us. We are our own gods." The new spiritual birth comes only when we acknowledge our shortcomings and invite Christ into our lives. The following is a suggested prayer that will lead to transformation and a new life.

Suggested Prayer

Dear God in heaven, I know I have sinned. I ask you to forgive every sin I have ever committed. I thank you that you provided a blood sacrifice for my sins through the death of your Son, Jesus Christ. I accept his blood as the blood sacrifice for my sins. I invite Jesus to come into my life and transform me. I thank you that according to John 1:12

I have the right to become your child because I believe in and confess your name. I will follow Jesus' example and enter the waters of baptism and come up a new creation—a son/daughter of God. Your Word says, "For you are all children of God through faith in Christ Jesus. And all who have been united with Christ in baptism have put on Christ, like putting on new clothes" (Gal. 3:26–27 NLT). Please help me to know you and to follow your ways. Amen.

The apostle, Paul, wrote to the Corinthians, "This means that anyone who belongs to Christ has become a new person. The old life is gone; a new life has begun! And all of this is a gift from God, who brought us back to himself through Christ. And God has given us this task of reconciling people to him" (2 Cor. 5:17–18 NLT). What an exciting promise! We are new creations. Think of the Bible as an instruction manual given to us with guidelines for living fulfilled lives.

Jesus' Baptism

Let's read the account of Jesus as he was starting his ministry when he walked over sixty miles from Galilee to the Jordan River to be baptized by John. "Then Jesus went from Galilee to the Jordan River to be baptized by John. But John tried to talk him out of it. 'I am the one who needs to be baptized by you,' he said, 'so why are you coming to me?' But Jesus said, 'It should be done, for we must carry out all that God requires.' So John agreed to baptize him. After his baptism, as Jesus came up out of the water, the heavens were opened and he saw the Spirit of God descending like a dove and settling on him" (Matt. 3:13–16 NLT).

Who can grasp why the sinless Son of God needed to carry out all that God requires? Only in eternity will we fully know why Jesus, who was totally sinless and completely righteous, regarded baptism as absolutely essential for himself. It is clear that Jesus set the example for all believers to follow throughout the ages.

I believe that anyone who wants to follow the Lord Jesus, and who is not hindered physically in some way, should follow his example and be baptized as a public witness to faith in Christ. The book of Acts records Ananias, a devout observer of the law and highly respected by the Jews, said to the newly converted Paul (Saul of Tarsus), "And now why are you waiting? Arise and be baptized, and wash away your sins, calling on the name of the Lord" (Acts 22:16 NKJV). The same refrain echoes today to anyone who has heard the word of salvation, believed the word of salvation, repented of their sins, and confessed Jesus Christ as Lord and Savior and asked him to transform their lives.

Rodney suggests the following steps to stand strong in the decision for Christ:

❖ Read the Bible daily, praying for insight and understanding (Acts 17:11)
❖ Pray about everything (Phil. 4:6–7, John 15:7)
❖ Unite with other God-honoring believers who accept that the Bible is the infallible (incapable of error) Word of God (Heb. 10:25)
❖ Cultivate a lifestyle of praise and worship (Ps. 107:1–2)
❖ Be a doer of the Word and not a hearer only (James 1:22)
❖ Live out your confession of Jesus Christ as Lord and Savior through the power of the Holy Spirit
❖ Talk of his gracious provision wherever the opportunity presents itself (Mark 16:15)

Choice to be Free

We can choose the pathway to freedom made possible by the blood sacrifice, death, and glorious resurrection of Jesus Christ. This pathway has a number of signposts along the way with keys to unlock the chains that bind. These keys are explored in the subsequent chapters of *Unshackled*, where you will see how the storytellers decided to walk in freedom. These truths (signposts) are given to us to live by to experience the full blessings of God in our lives. They are not always easy things to do, but God would not tell us to do something that was impossible. We have the power; we just need to be willing to act out of that power rather than out of our own desires and self-will. (One example of a truth we are to live by is to forgive those who have hurt us, as demonstrated in Rodney's dramatic account of his experience with his music teacher.)

Stories are included from those who have successfully embraced these basic principles for transforming their lives. Practical "how to" suggestions are contained within the text. Journey with me through the pages of this book. Read the stories for yourself so you can decide whether to take the road to freedom suggested, or continue on another path.

Reflection

1. How do you feel about the degree of freedom you are experiencing ?

2. What is holding you back from being all you can be?

3. What memories play over and over in your mind?

4. Do you want to live a joy-filled life fulfilling who you were created to be? Why or why not?

5. How will you consider the message of this book for your own life?

Chapter 2

DISCOVER YOUR TRUE IDENTITY

Have you heard that your Creator thinks you are wonderful and awesome? Do you know you are unique, one of a kind? Do you draw your opinion of yourself from what others have said about you? Many of us have had harsh words hurled at us which lodged deep within. Some have suffered unspeakable abuse, verbal and otherwise. Others have been abused by being deprived of love and affirmation from the authority figures in our lives.

Jenny tells her story: "'I wish you were never born!' were words hurled at me one day. Those words stung as they echoed through my head as an eleven-and-a-half-year-old child. I realize now that I had not done anything to deserve such words, but at the time I just knew there had to be some truth to what my mother said. I am now convinced she was mentally ill. She would make my two brothers and me sit and listen to her rant at us for hours on end over the most trivial things. Most of her tirades were just her frustrations being unleashed on three kids who were usually very obedient and wanted nothing more than to please their mother. If one of us would leave a sock on the floor we would endure hours of her wrath. Then she would stop right before our father came home from work. She was always impossible to please.

"My mother's childhood was marked with much pain, which was brought on by an alcoholic father. She remembers constant fighting between her parents. When she wasn't yelling at me she unloaded a lot of her emotional baggage. She shared how many times she feared being abandoned as a child. She chose to wallow in the past and feed a bitter root in her heart rather than nurture her only daughter. I carried the hurt and scars of years of her emotional and verbal abuse. It wasn't until I was in my twenties that God graciously allowed healing for me in this area of my life. God states that he will be a father to the fatherless, and he has also been a mother to the motherless. He was always there for me, comforting me and, in time, providing a mother for me I never had.

"In 1997, the Lord provided a godly woman who has become a dear friend and mentor to me. For over two years she met with me in my home on a regular basis. She gave me understanding about the many hurtful situations I had experienced at the hands of my mother. Then we would take it to God in prayer. Slowly the chains started dropping off—and they continue dropping off to this day as I pursue healthy ways to relate to my mother.

"I am now the mother of two daughters and two sons of my own. The years I should have had as a child with my mother I have chosen to have with my daughters. It is interesting that one of my daughters, in particular, has the same tendencies and idiosyncrasies that I had as a child and now have as an adult. As I watch her grow I am able to give her the nurture, love, and relationship that I never had with my mother. It is very healing to watch this sweet little girl do the same things that I did as a child. But instead of getting frustrated and verbally attacking her or belittling her, I am able to instruct her in wisdom so she will not continue making the same mistakes. I also am able to laugh as I watch her sweet spirit and know that she will never wonder if her mother wants her and loves her, or if her entrance into the world was a mistake. I know she will never be scarred by the verbal blows that cut to the heart. No child should ever experience that, let alone experience it from her mother. I treasure her laugh, her spirit, and her life! She is the child I should have been, confident, loving, and carefree. I have the unique privilege of watching this daughter and all of my children growing up free from the scars I suffered and confident of their true identity in the Lord."

Whether or not we were raised in "normal" homes, or in one like Jenny's, internal conflict rages within many of us over who we really are. Over the years we attempt in multiple ways to feed a gaping hole within. Drugs, alcohol, sexual addictions, the search for riches, and self-mutilation are examples of our attempt to fill that void.

True to Self

The expectations of others can also put us in chains if we are not alert enough to stop this from happening. We are all designed uniquely. No two people's fingerprints are the same, and no two people have the same talents. Our Creator made each of us with unique abilities, and we need to guard against others trying to mold us into their concept of what we should be. I remember a friend of my daughter's whose father insisted he go to the United States Military Academy at West Point. The young man was accepted and stayed there for a long miserable year before returning home feeling that he had disappointed his father. He never wanted to be a career military man in the first place, but his father had overruled his son's wishes. A year of his life was wasted, and he had severely disappointed and failed his father. And now what were the end results on his self-image?

Many of us do not take a direct path to our life work, hobbies, and interests. Fortunate is the person who knows the direction to take early in his or her life. Many of us have to try out a number of things before we find what we are designed to do. There are many widely available tests online—through guidance counselors, in books at Christian bookstores, or at places of worship—that can be effective at identifying our gifts and talents.

There are seasons in nature and there are seasons in life. We need to learn to embrace the season and not war against it. Nor do we need to tap our foot and wait impatiently for the next season. The Old Testament book of Ecclesiastes tells us there is a time and season for everything:

> There is a time for everything, and a season for every activity under heaven: a time to be born and a time to die, a time to plant and a time to uproot, a time to kill and a time to heal, a time to tear down and a time to build, a time to weep and a time to laugh, a time to mourn and a time to dance, a time to scatter stones and a time to gather them, a time to embrace and a time to refrain, a time to search and a time to give up, a time to keep and a time to throw away, a time to tear and a time to mend, a time to be silent and a time to speak, a time to love and a time to hate, a time for war and a time for peace.
> —3:1–8 NIV

It is wise to learn to enjoy the season we are in to the fullest. When we do that, we can move on when it is time to let it go.

One of the greatest breakthroughs in my life came when I learned to accept that I could not always do everything perfectly, and that I did not need to compare myself with others who were better than me in certain things. For example, I could not make a decent meringue pie in spite of lessons from my expert sister, Dot. I decided to buy meringue pies from the bakery instead of trying to bake them myself.

We may try pursuing various activities just because they are popular, but they may not really suit us or our abilities. Try to discern where you need to be stretched to learn something new, and where you are only pursuing it because you noticed someone else doing it. Don't be pulled into things by others. We can easily get into subtle competition without being aware of it. Just because a friend is interested in, and good at, a hobby or activity does not automatically mean it is right for us.

I think that in some ways men have a harder time being true to who God made them to be than women do. Men do not voice as much self-doubt as women. Instead, they can exhibit overbearing, dogmatic behavior. This may result in trying to exercise unhealthy control, especially over the women in their lives. Some men are the primary breadwinners for their families, which can cause pressure to perform in certain ways. They may be required to participate in social and sport activities as an extension of their jobs. Expectations are placed on them in the work environment that may conflict with the inner man's true self. In addition to job responsibilities, men also are responsible to guide their family in their belief system.

For men who are Christians, there are principles set forth in Scripture to guide them. Some have theorized that the father holds a greater role in the formation of a child's personality than the mother, although sometimes it is the mother who handles childcare on a day-to-day basis. All of the same pressures may apply for women who pursue careers.

It has been my observation that a woman's insecurity manifests itself as low self-esteem. Some of us women are constantly second-guessing and doubting ourselves. Men express insecurity in a different way. Some men want to dominate and always have all of the answers. Upon close observation, I have often found an insecure man behind this facade.

Some men have wives who constantly demean them and tear them down (and the converse is also true). Honoring, affirming, and respecting a mate is necessary for both wives and husbands. It takes a strong man to know who his Maker designed him to be and to be that person in spite of the numerous pressures to pigeonhole him. Both sexes may have the additional hardship of not having had a healthy role model as they grew up.

Inspiring and Affirming Each Other

I have found it good to observe the positive attributes in others and develop them in my own life. This is not copying others out of feelings of jealousy or inadequacy. We can be a great encouragement to each other by affirming the areas of strength we observe. On a number of occasions when I have paid a compliment to someone, they have responded, "I didn't know that about myself." Accept graciously the words spoken to you.

Many books have been written on why we should affirm our children and how we should do it. This is a vital part of parenting. The suggestions made for friends work as well with children. We should especially be aware of the "labels" we put on them. Just as we do with friends, we should encourage children to find what fits them. This can be an enjoyable adventure. Margie told her mother, "I tried so many different activities when I was growing up. I appreciate so much how patient you were with me." Her mother's helpful attitude enabled Margie to discover what she was interested in and where she excelled. It helped her embrace a lifework that truly suited her.

Pat had a difficult time when her instructor in college dealt her a devastating blow in journalism class. "I will never forget that fateful day when the instructor called me into his office during my first year as a college journalism student. All of my life I knew I could write well, and I always got good grades—not to mention that family and friends affirmed my writing gift as well. I had even won two writing essay contests when I was in elementary school and in junior high. One essay encouraged a young man who read it to live and not commit suicide.

"Naturally, I was sure the consultation with my professor was to tell me what a great job I was doing. As he began telling me what a great command I had in developing the theme of a story and carrying it through, I was beaming with joy and knew that his next words would be that my skills far exceeded what he was offering in his class.

"Instead came the blow: 'I don't understand something. It is obvious you have a great command of theme development, but I can't figure out why your grammar and syntax are so poor.' The beam of pride that glowed from my face turned into disbelief. I couldn't believe my ears. What in the world was he talking about? I had been a good writer all of my life and now this man implied I couldn't write! My mind was racing, and all I knew was that he had no idea what he was talking about. Yet, I sat and listened as he lowered the boom. 'If you were to stay in this class you would not pass. I recommend you go back and learn the basics. You can enroll in the introduction to writing class to improve your grammar.'

"I left that class devastated. I don't know how I made it home. Tears were streaming uncontrollably as I zoomed up the freeway. So many thoughts flooded my mind. He had to be a racist and just didn't want to see a young black woman succeed. White people always say blacks don't know English. How could I tell my family? Obtaining my degree in mass communications was critical for me to become a journalist. His words had just shattered my dreams.

"When I got home I went to my room and called a close friend. As I poured out my heart to her about the traumatic experience, she tried calming me down. Having her sympathetic ear helped as she suggested two possible solutions: I could drop out of school, or I could take the recommended introduction to writing class. I decided to take the class and prove him wrong.

"My first couple of sessions in the introductory writing class proved futile because the instructor quickly recognized I had problems with grammar. He recommended I take rudimentary classes to learn the basics. Now I was even more determined I would not give up. I would prove both of the teachers wrong.

"After repeatedly hearing I could not write, I became fearful of even trying. It would take forever. I feared others would find out I was not a good writer. Rather than having to endure the shame and humiliation of being told I could not write, I stopped writing and hid behind fear.

"I lived with this fear for twenty years. In June, 1998 I embraced Jesus as Lord and Savior. By this time I was consumed with fear. I sought God's help for the fear that plagued me and prevented me from having confidence in my capabilities. I was diligent in learning about fear and its underpinning causes. It is all consuming. If you entertain even a hairline crack it will seep into other areas in your life as well. I searched the Word of God and began applying Scriptures to overcome fear and give me a renewed mind. I prayed Romans 12:1–2 daily that I would not 'conform any longer to the pattern of this world, but be transformed by the renewing of [my] mind. Then [I] will be able to test and approve what God's will is—his good, pleasing and perfect will' (Rom. 12:2 NIV). I wanted God to transform me and give me a renewed mind to do his most perfect and acceptable will. I brought my fear out in the open. The more I revealed my fear of writing, the less power it had over me.

"After reading Isaiah 30:8, 'Now go and write down these words. Write them in a book. They will stand until the end of time as a witness' (NLT), I asked God to anoint my hands to write a book for this generation, as well as those to come, so others would know how to be set free to become all God created them to be. I quickly grasped the fact that as long as I allowed fear to rule I would not become all God had for my life. My journal writings went from, 'Lord deliver me' to 'I am not afraid.'

"The Word of God, prayer, and fasting helped me to overcome. Now I distribute written inspirational messages all across the country, and with God's grace I have written a soon-to-be released book. The anger I felt towards my instructor when he did not affirm what I knew my gift to be has now evolved into gratitude. Had he not pointed out my writing deficiencies, I never would have corrected the problem. Once I teamed up with God, he revealed that it was divinely appointed for the teacher to tell me what he did so that God could use my writing for his glory. My faith increased substantially. The words spoken by the instructor helped me to develop to the fullest the real me."

The Real Self

We must strip off the chains of who others think we should be and let God uncover and reveal the authentic man or woman inside. "If we don't find our personhood in Jesus Christ we will always be desperately prowling the world looking for someone else to heal us and make the bad go away."[1] "Finding the true center of our being is discovered in surrender to Christ."[2] Let the "real" person emerge.

We are all familiar with post-it notes. How often do we make notes to ourselves or others and then stick them places as reminders? As we travel through life, others put labels (stickers) on us by the words they speak. We can then become so covered up with all kinds of labels that often the real person cannot show through. We may start acting out the labels rather than being our true selves.

We have all experienced untrue or unflattering labels that have stuck. It is worth the time to take an inventory of what we have believed about ourselves over the years. Many of those were mere labels and had nothing to do with who we actually are. There are also good stickers that people will put on us. When we evaluate the words spoken about us, we learn to discern the truth. We discard the words that are destructive, learn from the ones that would help us, and accept the positive ones that affirm us and our special gifts.

Acceptance

The chains come off and great peace comes as we learn who our Creator made us to be. It is only when we accept ourselves as he made us that we settle into our own skin and reach our full potential. As we accept ourselves and become comfortable with who we are we become free to appreciate and call forth the talents of others with no spirit of jealousy. David's awe is expressed in the Bible when he writes, "Thank you for making me so wonderfully complex! Your workmanship is marvelous—how well I know it" (Ps. 139:14 NLT). This can be the heart song for all of us as God's creations. We know we are God's treasures, and we know we were knit together in our mother's womb. We are "fearfully and wonderfully made" (Ps. 139:14 NIV). Our frames were not hidden from God when we were made in the secret place and woven together in the depths of the earth. We are made whole and complete as we find the true center of our being and we surrender to Christ. We discover the unique design God put within us and allow that true self to come forth transformed.

"With divine fingers God shapes every person in the womb into an image and form like His own. Each precisely etched embryo is a person whom God has laid out for his own use from eternity past. Each of us has been known and loved since the beginning of time even before the world was made."[3]

There is no insignificant place of service. The most humble task may have a profound influence in someone's life. Jesus told us that even a cup of water given in his name is the same as serving him. Many are tucked away in obscure, unrecognized places serving faithfully year after year. Great will be their reward!

We should examine the roots of any insecurity that keeps us chained. We can ask God to pull out those roots and heal the area so that the chains fall off. God has provided many competent counselors, pastors, and laypeople to bring emotional wholeness. We learn from our mistakes, we learn that failure is not necessarily defeat, and that neither is defeat necessarily failure. Both failure and defeat give us the opportunity to try again until we succeed. No one should base their value as human beings on mistakes made in life.

While we can draw encouragement and strength from each other, we also must learn not to depend on others for our sense of identity and self-worth. We can learn from wise older men and women who have blazed a trail before us.

It is helpful to learn and practice a gentle embrace from the inside out as we appreciate and draw on our uniqueness. In addition, we encourage our family and friends in their special talents with no envy or jealousy.

My friend Sally says that, "as a young woman in my thirties and forties I never felt like I measured up. I believed I was not quite good enough and was not secure in who I was. I was afraid of failure and criticism, and I was extremely competitive even with myself. There were some tragic and lonely times throughout those years. I was in the 'valley' several times, but now I realize God was with me and my walk with him became closer. A Scripture that really helped me was, 'If God is for us, who can ever be against us?'" (Rom. 8:31 NLT). This is a scripture we can use to encourage others as well as ourselves.

Sally continues, "I began to study God's Word more and to search for the reason I felt so worthless. I tried to be honest in assessing my shortcomings and failures. Scripture revealed his unconditional love which began to sink into my inner woman. I started to accept myself as God made me. After many years I have learned to depend on God for my sense of security and self-worth. I have a special place with him just as all of his children do."

Jean shared this story, which beautifully illustrates Sally's conclusion: "When Ralph and I were dating, my son Mike was about six years old. One day we were in the car with Ralph's two teen-age daughters, Patsy and Jan, and Mike stuck his head between us in the front seat. He declared, 'Mom, I think Ralph loves Patsy more than Jan.' The car became extremely quiet. I immediately asked God for wisdom, since I have none apart from him.

"These were the words which came to me: 'No, Mike, that's impossible. When you love someone, that person has a special place in your heart. It would be impossible for Jan to climb in Patsy's place in Ralph's heart, or for Patsy to climb into Jan's place. Each has her own special place in her Daddy's heart.' This insight has helped our family many times over. We each have a special place in God's heart, and no one can usurp our place. Thank you God."

Suggested Prayer

Dear God, help me see myself as you see me. Help me to recognize and use my talents. I aspire to be the "best me" I can be. Grant me courage to step out in unfamiliar territory. I affirm that "I can do everything through Christ, who gives me strength" (Phil. 4:13 NLT). In the name of Jesus I pray. Amen.

Reflection

1. How well do you feel you know yourself?

2. Are you jealous of others? Why?

3. How can you celebrate victories in your friends' lives?

4. What would you like to achieve in your life?

Chapter 3

FREEDOM FROM TORMENTING THOUGHTS

Are you bombarded with inappropriate thoughts? Do you see a person of the opposite sex and think of romantic, inappropriate encounters with them? Do you look at other people and immediately judge their behavior? Do your thoughts hold you captive?

Bill shared his story about getting freedom from worrisome thoughts: "My struggle was with worry. It went like this: What if? What about? Sitting at a stop light I worried that I couldn't recall what I had been worried about. It was a false sense of control—a type of contingency planning. I had an obsessive compulsive/anxiety disorder. To reduce anxiety my OCD caused me to do things over and over. I would check the stove repeatedly to make sure it was off, or set the alarm clock over and over at night. The most extreme act was checking to see if the cat had drowned in the toilet.

"I had a huge growth opportunity and so I turned for help to the One to whom I had entrusted my life thirteen years before. It came down to trusting that God was able to take care of me and whether or not I would rely on his absolute goodness. I discovered these two truths: First, God is in charge. His Word tells me in Psalm 9:10 that 'those who know your name trust in you, for you, O Lord, do not abandon those who search for you' (NLT). Isaiah 26:3 assures me the Lord will 'keep in perfect peace all who trust in you, all whose thoughts are fixed on you!' (NLT). My mind had to be renewed in order to change my focus. Second, God is good. He isn't out to hurt me. He wants what is best for me.

"Sometimes I can't see the good, but I am convinced now that there is always good in his direction of my paths. Ezekiel 33:11 says, 'I take no pleasure in the death of wicked people. I only want them to turn from their wicked ways so they can live. Turn! Turn from your wickedness, O people of Israel! Why should you die?' (NLT).

"God sent his Son to die for me because he loves me. Sometimes I have to fight back the temptation to worry about things and I have to ask God to help me think on truth and leave deception behind."

Larry had a different challenge with his thoughts. "At first glance 'scrupulous' would seem to be a good character trait as it indicates careful attention to what is right or proper. It also is defined by conscientious honesty characterized by precision, care, and exactness. But through wounds, fear of reprisal, and perfectionism, it takes on a hideous form in what is known in clinical terms as OCD—Obsessive Compulsive Disorder. Being overly scrupulous brought to my sensitive, artistic nature a false sense of guilt, a false sense of responsibility, an excessive sense of responsibility, and much doubt in everything. I also dealt with fear and insecurity, and a great need to seek people's approval. All of these traits describe me in my life journey. My sensitive nature caused me to become more easily hurt and pained than those born with a stronger disposition and who are less sensitive.

"As I commit my life to the One who created me, I am learning to receive something our instruction manual (the Bible) calls *grace*. God is slowly healing and transforming me into his image and into the whole person he created me to be. He has used my pain to help me grow close and he has burned away my self-sufficiency, pride, hatred, lust, and even fear. The process is dreadfully slow, but it is sure.

FREEDOM FROM
TORMENTING THOUGHTS

"I cling to the fact that God will never leave me or forsake me. Hebrews 13:5 promises that because of God's great love for me, 'Never will I leave you; never will I forsake you' (NIV). God is very scrupulous in the best way possible."

Each of us has our own unique struggles in our thought life. We can feel battered with thoughts that are not healthy and that do us great harm, causing our minds to be obsessed with whatever our weakness happens to be. Many of us have problems with lustful, unhealthy sexual thoughts. Others of us may be tempted to steal, lie, or have any number of other areas of bondage. Some have problems in interpersonal relationships such as thinking that others do not like us, or we hold grudges. The good news is that *the thoughts are not the sin unless we nurse them and fantasize over them.* It is acting on them that is wrong. Many of us have stayed in the shadow of shame because we did not understand the difference between the thought and acting on it.

For those of us who choose to ask God to transform us, he gives us the power to overcome these thoughts. We can refuse them when they come knocking on the door of our mind. We do not have to be victims. Tommy Newberry reveals the secret to a joy-filled life in his book, *The 4:8 Principle*, which is based on the text of Philippians 4:8: "Finally, brothers, whatever is true, whatever is noble, whatever is right, whatever is pure, whatever is lovely, whatever is admirable—if anything is excellent or praiseworthy—think about such things" (NIV). He outlines what we should focus on in our thought life. "Philippians 4:8 reflects very crisply the nature and character of God, who himself is true, noble, just, pure, lovely, and of good report."[1] Newberry suggests we check our thoughts by these qualities.

Thoughts that are allowed free reign turn into imaginations, and imaginations eventually take over and set up strongholds. "An imagination is intent to do something about what you have been thinking. A stronghold is when the choice is not yours anymore, but you have submitted your will to the thought."[2] Strongholds control us if we do not control them. It is far easier to stop the destructive thought before it "sets up house."

Another challenging area for me lies in interpersonal relationships. This may be as simple as meeting a person and immediately thinking they do not like me. It often involves second-guessing others instead of accepting what they say without trying to decide if they really meant what they said. It was a tremendous relief when I made up my mind to believe that people mean what they say. If, per chance, they don't, they bear the responsibility for misrepresenting their beliefs. It was very freeing for me when I decided to follow this approach in my dealings with others. I decided to accept what they say and not try to figure out if they meant it or if they had a secret motive.

I was chained in my thought life until I learned to cast down destructive thoughts that led me into wrong behaviors or attitudes. The person who has chosen to follow Christ can check their thoughts to see if they line up with what God's Word says. Many of us do not fully understand that we have the power to do this. We may pray against destructive thoughts by asking God to protect us from them, and that is very appropriate. But we may not have understood that it is our responsibility to resist these thoughts at the threshold of our minds. God has already given us the power to do this through his Spirit living in us.

Scripture instructs us that "we are human, but we don't wage war as humans do. We use God's mighty weapons, not worldly weapons, to knock down the strongholds of human reasoning and to destroy false arguments. We destroy every proud obstacle that keeps people from knowing God. We capture their rebellious thoughts and teach them to obey Christ" (2 Cor. 10:3–5 NLT).

We discover God's nature as it is revealed through his written Word and through Jesus who is the Word made flesh. As we study the life of Christ when he lived on earth we have a picture of the heart of God towards his creation. The gospel of John tells us, "Anyone who has seen me has seen the Father!" (14:9b NLT). In addition, we have the written record of God's dealings with human beings throughout the whole of Scripture. Some of us have to overcome wrong images that have been planted in us about the nature of God. Beyond this we can develop an increased understanding of the divine ways if we accept Christ and his guidance for our lives. It is wise to study the Scriptures and to live in the wisdom they provide.

It is important to note that we should never accept life experiences and impressions as truth if they are not consistent with the Word of God as revealed in Scripture and in the life of Jesus. The apostle Paul's message in 2 Corinthians is further clarified in *The Message*: "The tools of our trade aren't for marketing or manipulation, but they are for demolishing that entire massively corrupt culture. We use our powerful God-tools for smashing warped philosophies, tearing down barriers erected against the truth of God, fitting every loose thought and emotion and impulse into the structure of life shaped by Christ" (10:3–5). This applies to our own thoughts as well as the thoughts we encounter in those with whom we converse. We check to be sure the thoughts are not in conflict with the written Word of God.

Types of Thoughts

Four specific areas offer challenges to many of us in our thought life.

1. Feelings of self-doubt and defeat. These are thoughts against ourselves, causing us to not fully acknowledge, embrace, and walk in our God-given abilities. Comparing ourselves with others is a very common trap.
2. Thoughts involving other people with the temptation to take offense, pass judgments, or react with ungodly mean-spirited behavior.
3. Impure thoughts involving acts of sin (among these are worry, fear, envy, bitterness, discouragement, lust, pride, lying, and anger). Many of us have continuing battles with ungodly thoughts coming across our minds. We feel guilty and helpless.
4. Thoughts that cause us to doubt God's love and provision for our every need or the needs of others. These thoughts war against the very character of God. One of Satan's main attacks on believers in Jesus Christ is to try to get us to doubt the character of God the Father. This happened to the first woman in the Garden of Eden. Satan planted doubts in her mind about her Creator. Doubt in the goodness of God has continued to plague our race ever since. Satan is still trying to subtly interject into our minds the question, "Did God really say?" and to get us to believe that "You will not surely die" (Gen. 3:1, 4 NIV).

Satan is the Father of Lies. As such, he tries to appeal to our independent and rebellious nature. This nature is often so buried within us that we are unaware it is lying dormant and waiting to spring into action. Scripture tells us, "For the world offers only a craving for physical pleasure, a craving for everything we see, and pride in our achievements and possessions. These are not from the Father, but are from this world" (1 John 2:16 NLT).

The five God-given senses of the human body (seeing, hearing, smelling, tasting, and touching) offer entrance to the threshold of the mind. In addition, thoughts spring from within us, or they are planted there by the actions or words of others. Old, unresolved wounds offer a nesting place for unhealthy thoughts.

I believe that thoughts are triggered by these four sources:

1. Our own minds (past experiences, preconceived ideas, wrong teaching, things we take in through the senses)
2. The words or actions of others
3. The Evil One, Satan
4. God

As we grow in our transformed thinking, this order should be reversed so that God, through our knowledge of Scripture and his character, rules our thoughts more and more. Words of Scripture stored up in our minds, as well as impressions from the indwelling Spirit of God, will start to transform our thoughts.

The Bible tells us we have the mind of Christ: "'Who can know the LORD's thoughts? Who knows enough to teach him?' But we understand these things, for we have the mind of Christ" (1 Cor. 2:16 NLT). But we have to choose to let that mind determine our thoughts and behavior instead of our un-renewed mind, which may have controlled us for many years.

Difference in Thought and Sin

Many Christians have been deceived into thinking that sin lies in having an ungodly thought flash across our minds. We feel defeated and helpless because we do not understand that the thought itself is not sin. The important thing is what we do with the thought. If we let it in, it leads to sin and shame. Doubt, anxiety, anger, and nervousness show up and disrupt our physical and spiritual rest. We are not responsible for the thoughts that flash across our minds unless we are exposing ourselves to situations that trigger these thoughts.

Sin is present only if we allow the thought to stay; we wrap our minds around it and allow ourselves to be snared by it. We are responsible for controlling our thoughts through the power of the indwelling Holy Spirit. We can follow Jesus' pattern in the fourth chapter of Matthew and speak aloud the appropriate scripture to our adversary and tempter.

Common Areas of Challenge

One area where Satan is busy at work is in dividing Christian brothers and sisters as well as sowing discord with non-Christians. We are all in varying degrees of spiritual growth and immaturity, hopefully moving on toward maturity in Christ. We need to extend mercy to each other and refuse to be offended. "Great peace have they who love Your law; nothing shall offend them or make them stumble" (Ps. 119:165 AMPLIFIED). Pride in our own knowledge and spiritual superiority can provide an entrance for offense taking root. If we are to walk in victory we need to learn to examine ourselves as these situations arise. Offense is addressed further in a subsequent chapter.

Many of us have experienced the workings of Satan in our relationships with others. Charlie and Dot felt shackled by the unloving way they were treated in their church, and this resulted in their leaving after much prayer and struggle. Previously, their pastor had approached them for ordination. Charlie and Dot accepted and looked forward to developing in ministry skills. However, their church assignments and duties, including heavy administrative oversight of the church building, did not leave time to develop as ministers.

On one occasion Dot and Charlie were asked to submit a mini-sermon which would highlight the need for loyalty to the pastor. This was a subtle way of pointing out that they lacked loyalty—which was untrue and deeply hurtful.

Dot and Charlie had the opportunity to put into practice forgiveness and not taking offense. This was hard, but they were determined not to return evil for evil, but instead good for evil. They wanted to show love and they did so even to the point of apologizing to the pastor. They had to constantly choose not to be offended by the way they were treated. They were guided by Paul's counsel in Galatians 5:1, "So Christ has truly set us free. Now make sure that you stay free, and don't get tied up again in slavery to the law" (NLT). This is a caution for any who may be in a controlling church where the leadership rules with a heavy hand and does not allow for individual giftings to be developed. This is an example of the insecurities of a leader keeping someone shackled until he or she breaks free of a controlling, manipulative spirit.

Worry is a constant challenge for many Christians. We pray over situations but continue to hold on to them. We may not really release them to God and trust him to work them out. The chain of worry can really bind us. Thanks be to God we are not left hopeless in the face of our temptation to worry. We follow James 4:7–8: "So humble yourselves before God. Resist the devil, and he will flee from you. Come close to God, and God will come close to you" (NLT).

I have found fear and worry are like twins who are usually inseparable. Both are irrational. It has helped me to expose them by recognizing and admitting that they are present when they surface.

I Am Learning To:

❖ Guard my eyes and ears and pray for discernment and protection over them, knowing that I am responsible for that to which I expose myself ("Guard your heart above all else, for it determines the course of your life," Prov. 4:23 NLT).

❖ Examine my thoughts and take ungodly ones captive ("We use God's mighty weapons, not worldly weapons, to knock down the strongholds of human reasoning and to destroy false arguments.

We destroy every proud obstacle that keeps people from knowing God. We capture their rebellious thoughts and teach them to obey Christ," 2 Cor. 10:4–5 NLT).

❖ Let offenses find no lodging place in my spirit. ("Let us not become conceited, or provoke one another, or be jealous of one another," Gal. 5:26 NLT).

❖ Follow Jesus' example. When he spoke to Satan in the wilderness, he said, "It is written" (Matt. 4:4, Matt. 4:6, Matt. 4:7). I am to know and use the scripture that applies to my temptations. Satan is defeated when the Word of God is spoken aloud.

❖ Know my individual weaknesses and be on guard ("Then you will experience God's peace, which exceeds anything we can understand. His peace will guard your hearts and minds as you live in Christ Jesus," Phil. 4:7 NLT).

❖ Draw on the power of the Holy Spirit. He dwells in all who have asked to be transformed and have experienced the new birth ("So I say, let the Holy Spirit guide your lives. Then you won't be doing what your sinful nature craves," Gal. 5:16 NLT).

Four Steps to Victory

In a pamphlet entitled *A Study of the Mind*, Anabel Gillham identifies four steps to victory in our thought life: reckon (I prefer the word recognize), refuse, remember, and rest.

These steps are for the one who has chosen to be transformed by following Christ.

STEP 1: RECOGNIZE

For victory in the thought life, examine the thought to see where it originated. Check it according to the first piece of the armor that God provided for the followers of Christ—the belt of truth and the protection found in the breastplate of God's righteousness (Eph. 6:14). Is the thought true? Does it line up with what God's Word says? What triggered the thought? Will it bring glory to God? How would God want me to think about this? Is it a thought that promotes or hinders me walking free of chains?

Step 2: Refuse

For wrong thoughts, do not allow them entrance. If an intruder tried to gain entrance to our physical house, our attitude would be "Stop!" Likewise we are to say "stop" to an intruder into the thought life. Refuse it in the name of Jesus through the power of the Holy Spirit who lives in all who have decided to follow Jesus. The undesirable thought can be stopped at the threshold of one's mind when it first comes knocking to gain entrance. Do not wait until it implants itself and gains expression through inappropriate actions. If the thought is not consistent with Scripture we are never to accept it.

Step 3: Remember

"Likewise you also, reckon yourselves to be dead indeed to sin, but alive to God in Christ Jesus our Lord" (Rom. 6:11b NKJV).

Consider the provision of victory over sin which Jesus' death on the cross provided through his blood sacrifice. Jesus' blood provided a protection for the believer to use against ungodly thoughts. We claim, believe, and experience by faith the blood of Jesus over and around our minds. This is in the supernatural realm. Jesus' death defeated Satan so that God's followers can have victory in the thought life.

Strength comes by remembering that we are in Christ and Christ lives in us in the form of the Holy Spirit. Sin originates in the thought life, which is the gateway to the human spirit, body, and soul. We have divine help for our thought life through Jesus Christ.

Step 4: Rest

Rest in the victory. "We know that our old sinful selves were crucified with Christ so that sin might lose its power in our lives. We are no longer slaves to sin. For when we died with Christ we were set free from the power of sin" (Rom. 6:6–7 NLT). I am in Christ. He is in me!

For some of us it is a lifelong discipline and continuing challenge to cast off chains of worry. We save ourselves much grief when we follow Philippians 4:6–7, which encourages Christians with the words: "Don't worry about anything; instead, pray about everything. Tell God what you need, and thank him for all he has done. Then you will experience

God's peace, which exceeds anything we can understand. His peace will guard your hearts and minds as you live in Christ Jesus" (NLT).

Focusing the Mind

The apostle Paul wrote, "Don't copy the behavior and customs of this world, but let God transform you into a new person by changing the way you think. Then you will learn to know God's will for you, which is good and pleasing and perfect" (Rom. 12:2 NLT). In other words, we are not to be ruled by feelings! It is possible to control the focus of the mind by using the belt of truth, which involves the knowledge and recognition of the appropriate scriptural truth for the situation we are facing. The sword of the Spirit, which is the word of God and part of the whole armor of God, is speaking the Word of Truth to the misconceptions arising from within ourselves (we are often our own worst enemy) or put there by our adversary, Satan. The believer is not helpless in the face of defeating thoughts. Satan is stopped by the Word of God, if it is spoken in faith. The Word is our offensive weapon.

Consider the story of the blood applied to the doorpost at the Passover. The destroyer was halted at the door upon which the blood of the sacrificial lamb had been applied. "On that night I will pass through the land of Egypt and strike down every firstborn son and firstborn male animal in the land of Egypt. I will execute judgment against all the gods of Egypt, for I am the LORD! But the blood on your doorposts will serve as a sign, marking the houses where you are staying. When I see the blood, I will pass over you. This plague of death will not touch you when I strike the land of Egypt" (Exod. 12:12–13 NLT).

Jesus is our Passover Lamb who provides protection against the entrance of tormenting thoughts. Jesus bled as the thorns were forced into his flesh. That blood coursed down over his head and is a picture of the sacrifice he provided for his followers to have peace. Several scriptures attest to the fact that the crucified Christ is our peace and that he paid for that peace by hanging on the cross. One of them is, "But he was pierced for our rebellion, crushed for our sins. He was beaten so we could be whole. He was whipped so we could be healed" (Isa. 53:5 NLT).

Scripture offers guidance for checking thoughts. In his letter to the Philippians, Paul says, "And now dear brothers and sisters, let me say one more thing as I close this letter. Fix your thoughts on what is true and honorable and right. Think about things that are pure and lovely and admirable. Think about things that are excellent and worthy of praise" (4:8 NLT).

David Jeffares, a minister and counselor from Lexington, Kentucky, shares the idea of giving our minds to the Lord in the form of a prayer:

> Lord, today I surrender and make a full offering to you of my mind. I confess to you that I have followed my mind in the past, and it has been a battlefield and at times a war zone. I have become so attacked in my mind that I have allowed myself in the past to believe the lies of the Evil One and I have surrendered to the unclean and destructive thoughts of my mind. I will not do that any longer, Heavenly Father; by your revealed and holy Word, you have promised to keep me in perfect peace when I focus my mind continually on you (Isaiah 26:3). I surrender my mind to you. I request formally at this time that you in your great wisdom and power give me the mind of Christ Jesus. I ask you to cleanse my mind from all uncleanness, and give me the mastery of my thoughts. In Jesus' name. Amen.

Reflection

1. Do you have control over your thoughts? Why or why not?

2. Would it embarrass you to have your thoughts thrown up on a public screen?

3. What do you do to stop unhealthy thoughts?

4. Would it feel good to be rid of some of your thoughts? How so?

Chapter 4

CHAINS OF OFFENSE

D o you struggle with people who just tick you off big time? Are you constantly having to deal with feelings of being ignored, misunderstood, or insulted by others? To live as free men and women it is crucial to learn to guard against taking offense. Scripture teaches us that "Great peace have they who love Your law; nothing shall offend them or make them stumble" (Ps. 119:165 AMPLIFIED). And "Hatred stirs up quarrels, but love makes up for all offenses" (Prov. 10:12 NLT).

The Source Behind Conflicts

The self-will and the world we live in sets a climate for being offended by what others say or do. What others say and do may keep us in a state of agitation and unrest. In addition, the Evil One (Satan) loves to get us all stirred up and in conflict with each other. For those of us who have decided to let Jesus Christ transform us, we have a power source within us that helps us to overlook offenses. That power source helps us practice the Scripture's teaching not to take offense. Joyce Meyer, a well-known Bible teacher, stated in one of her 2005 (no month given) newsletters that "I have found that one of the Devil's most subtle and dangerous weapons in these last days is the spirit of offense. Offenses are stumbling stones—they hinder our spiritual progress—and I believe Satan is using offense in a major way to prevent people from growing in their relationship with Christ."

Our common enemy, Satan, is trying hard to cause conflict between members of the human race, especially Christians, as well as people of other faiths or even of no faith. He fuels disagreements and misunderstandings. He distorts our interpretation of the actions and words of others and puts inflammatory thoughts in our minds. These thoughts then cloud our hearing and vision. He delights in getting us into isolation and self-pity. Sometimes this is in response to real or perceived slights, as well as direct assaults on our personhood.

Dealing With Unforgiveness/Hurt Feelings

Many of us have dealt with major issues of unforgiveness and hurt feelings that take root in our spirit when we receive offense. A subsequent chapter on forgiveness addresses this in detail and gives steps I have found helpful when forgiving others. One approach for me is to refuse the offense when it first comes knocking on the door of my mind. This is a choice, but it is a choice that does not come naturally. Adam was the first man in the human race, and his choice to disregard God's instructions affected all of us coming after him. We are all in the fallen line of rebels, and we are born with self-will natures. We are all the products of wounded, imperfect family lines, imperfect life histories, imperfect friends, and imperfect relationships. We are all flawed! It helped me tremendously when I made the decision to live comfortably with imperfect people, myself included.

In addition, we all have an enemy roaring around like a lion, seeking those whom he can devour (1 Pet. 5:8). If we can get a clear, firm vision of him as the force behind our challenges with others, we will be ready to walk away in victory as opportunities to take offense present themselves.

Joyce Meyer also revealed that in the Greek (the language in which the New Testament was written) the word for *offense* originally referred to the part of an animal trap that held the bait. In the same way, the devil lures us into becoming offended at something, and then that offense grows into bitterness and steals our joy. She says, "We have heard the phrase that someone 'took offense.' That is exactly right. The devil offers it to us, and many times—even unknowingly—we walk into his trap and take it."

A lady related to me how she sat across the supper table from her husband one night and was able to resist the challenge to engage him in conflict in response to things he was saying. First she reminded herself of the stress he may have encountered at work. Then she discerned that there was an evil spiritual force (not her husband) trying to fuel the situation to harass her. Understanding that challenges often come from evil spiritual forces provides a great help in ignoring potentially offensive situations.

A young high school boy sat down at the kitchen table one day after school and said to his mother, "I am in a bad mood. I am not mad at you, something happened at school." Then he related the incident. Making a straightforward statement about what was bothering him was a very mature approach, and it spared the mother the anxiety of wondering what, if anything, she had done to provoke a bad mood.

When we are with those we can trust, it is wise to admit our feelings, and be open and transparent. It requires spiritual discernment to know with whom we can share our deep heart cries, dreams, and aspirations.

Our Creator is not through perfecting any of us until we exit this world. Our sins are removed when our "spirit man" is transformed by Christ, but the temptation is ever-present to fall back into old patterns. Walking according to godly principles has to be worked into our actions and behaviors as we are trained to recognize the difference between right and wrong. The writer of Hebrews says that "solid food is for the mature, who by constant use have trained themselves to distinguish good from evil" (5:14 NIV). This means we learn how to choose the right action, and this training comes as we obey the prompting of the Spirit of God who lives in those who have chosen to follow his way. In addition, we check to be sure our behavior lines up with Scripture.

I try to remember that others have their own set of wounds and immaturity. This helps me extend mercy to them in challenging situations so I do not let offenses take root. We are all "walking wounded" in some area of our lives. "See to it that no one misses the grace of God and that no bitter root grows up to cause trouble and defile many" (Heb. 12:15 NIV).

Sherry related the following story that many may face in our society as sexual standards and boundaries become more and more relaxed. "My challenge began with a 2:30 AM phone call which startled and awakened me out of a sound sleep. The voice on the other end was the mother of my son's girlfriend, Linda, who had just broken the news that she was pregnant by my son. The news fell like hot burning coals as I was told Sam was threatening to commit suicide if Linda did not agree to have an abortion. I started crying out to the Lord asking for his peace. I reassured Linda's mother they had made the right decision not to abort the baby. I spoke to Linda and expressed love for her and told her I would be praying for her.

"After some time I was able to reach my son by phone. The suicide threat was averted. Over the next seven months I prayed for peace, good health, safe delivery, and that Linda would be healed of her broken heart due to my son's decision not to marry her.

"My first grandchild was born in a city some distance away. What should have been a joyous, celebratory time was a bittersweet moment. The exhilaration of being a grandparent for the first time was tinged with deep sadness and marred by the circumstances. Two weeks later I visited Linda and the baby. Relationships were strained because of the tug-of-war between Linda and my son—who was being denied access to his baby daughter. My protective, motherly instincts tried to surface. I considered taking legal steps to ensure visitation rights for both my son and myself. A lawyer was encouraging me to do so, saying if I didn't settle this in the beginning I would never see the child.

"But I felt God tell me, 'Sherry, if you choose to go the legal route you will never be able to repair the damage that will be done, and you will lose the child. If you choose to walk by my love it will be the bridge to close the gap between you.' I had to understand it would take a deep committed love. I was tempted many times to go back to the legal route, but I always remembered the thought I had of the healing pathway. I decided to walk by love. The thirteenth chapter of 1 Corinthians defines what this love should look like:

> If I speak in the tongues of men and of angels, but have not love, I am only a resounding gong or a clanging cymbal. If I have the gift of prophecy and can fathom all mysteries and all knowledge, and if I have a faith that can move mountains, but have not love, I am nothing. If I give all I possess to the poor and surrender my body to the flames, but have not love, I gain nothing. Love is patient, love is kind. It does not envy, it does not boast, it is not proud. It is not rude, it is not self-seeking, it is not easily angered, it keeps no record of wrongs. Love does not delight in evil but rejoices with the truth. It always protects, always trusts, always hopes, always perseveres. Love never fails. But where there are prophecies, they will cease; where there are tongues, they will be stilled; where there is knowledge, it will pass away. For we know in part and we prophesy in part, but when perfection comes, the imperfect disappears. When I was a child, I talked like a child, I thought like a child, I reasoned like a child. When I became a man, I put childish ways behind me. Now we see but a poor reflection as in a mirror; then we shall see face to face. Now I know in part; then I shall know fully, even as I am fully known. And now these three remain: faith, hope and love. But the greatest of these is love. (NIV)

This has been my pattern as I have lived out this extremely difficult situation trying to be a grandmother to my illegitimate, bi-racial grandchild. This was possible only through the power of the Holy Spirit who lives within me.

"Challenges continue to arise, compounded by the fact that my son married someone else eight months later and is now the father of another little girl. Making the decision to walk in the love principles from Scripture has enabled me to know my granddaughter, visit her, and be a part of her life. In fact I pray often for a godly man to be a husband for Linda. I ask for one who will love my granddaughter with a pure godly love. My choosing to walk in love has also made it possible for my son to be a part of the baby's life.

"I did not choose to take up Sam's offense in the situation or take up offense against Linda, nor did I encourage Sam in any feelings of being offended. The Lord has honored my choice to walk by his principles and not the 'go to war over this' tendency which seems second nature to many of us."

Practical Help

"For we are not fighting against people made of flesh and blood, but against the evil rulers and authorities of the unseen world, against those mighty powers of darkness who rule this world, and against wicked spirits in the heavenly realms" (Eph. 6:12 NLT). As we sense situations brewing we need to remind ourselves that Satan is trying to shoot arrows at us and that he is the source behind many negative thoughts and events. We can repel his attacks when we speak aloud the Word of God, which encourages us to not take offense.

It helps to choose to obey Scripture if we remember that Satan is trying to poison our walk with the heavenly Father through battles with others. Conflicts can lead to the deadly enemy of bitterness. When I recognize the source of the temptation to embrace offense, then I can deal Satan a mortal blow in the situation. I can refuse to act on the temptation to be offended.

It is important to note that the practical application of this does not mean denying our feelings or emotions. I take those to God in prayer after dealing with the immediate challenge to take offense. Scripture tells us, "People with good sense restrain their anger; they earn esteem by overlooking wrongs" (Prov. 19:11 NLT).

One of the reasons we are tempted to take offense is because of our expectations of others. When people do not say what we want to hear, or do what we think they should, then the opportunity to be offended presents itself. Frances Frangipane states: "I discuss issues and expectations with those close to me, but the weight of my expectation is not on others, but upon myself to be Christ-like and sensitive to those around me. I put a premium upon enjoying the uniqueness of others, sincerely thanking them for their contribution to my life."[1]

Judi has an interesting story, with which any parent can sympathize, of her struggle with offense. "When my son's wife left him because he was diagnosed with melanoma, I became hurt, disappointed, and extremely angry. I just wanted to lock her up because of the hurt she had caused my son and me as well. Just lock her up and hold her responsible! Never forget or forgive, never write off the injustice—make her pay. I would build a prison, large and strong, where she could never escape. She didn't deserve parole. Just lock her up and keep the only key in a very safe place.

"The only problem was I had to stay at the jail to guard her. I couldn't move on, I couldn't rise above. I couldn't pursue my dreams or goals. I had built the jail; now I was the jailer. The Lord revealed to me that there wasn't much difference between being in or out. Walls were walls. I didn't want to be a jailer. I had to open the cell and offer a complete pardon. I had to choose to forgive and forget and dismiss all of the charges. I had to let her out and let God work his own justice. I had to let her out and tear down the jail. It was an eyesore anyway. That's when I knew I had to decide whether I wanted to spend the rest of my life looking at stark prison walls or looking at mighty oceans of mercy. That's when forgiveness came. I am happy to report that my son survived the cancer."

Kate shared her struggle with another sticky family issue: "The day that I had dreaded—the day that I prayed would never come—arrived as unexpectedly and unwelcome as ever. In my hand was a letter from my daughter telling me she was engaged to be married … to a black man. I took great pride in raising my four daughters to be godly women. I had a perfect picture of what their lives should look like. This picture just did not fit.

"For three years I fought Darlene on the issue of inter-racial dating. I was devastated to learn that she preferred dating black men over white men. My husband and I tried desperately to reason with her. Marriage is tough enough without dealing with differences in race or ethnic background. We assured her we were not racist. We encouraged her to work, socialize, and even worship with people of other races. But we never encouraged her to marry another race.

"What I had hoped was a passing phase with Darlene became a hard reality when she took a job in the town where her fiancé lived. The anger I felt toward her frightened me. Out of my hurt, I became indifferent to her. Many times when she called, I would not answer the phone. I did not even want to acknowledge her anymore as my daughter. In the midst of my anger, hurt, and resentment, I knew that what I was feeling was wrong. Why could I not accept this situation? Why was I struggling so? This young man my daughter loved was a devoted and faithful follower of Christ. He came from a wonderful Christian home. He wanted to serve the Lord in ministry. He was everything a mother would want for her daughter—except that his skin was a different color. Praying, pleading, crying, and bargaining with God got me nowhere. 'Please God,' I prayed, 'break them up. That would be such a miracle.' Yet, even as I prayed these words, I knew that the bigger miracle would be to change me.

"I don't know exactly when it happened, but slowly, and very surely, the binding chains began to drop off. When I was finally able to ask Darlene and Dick for forgiveness and give them my blessing, I knew a mighty work had been done. I could not take any credit for the change in me which I had experienced firsthand.

"The struggle was intense and the Lord had a firm grip on me, and I knew I must yield my will in this. I was like a butterfly in a cocoon struggling and struggling to break free. It took a long time, and a lot of time spent in prayer, before I got the victory. But it did come as surely as day follows night. It was the dark night of my soul, but God did not leave or forsake me while I struggled to allow him to free me."

Suggestions I Find Helpful For Victory

- ❖ I remind myself that I have an enemy fueling the offense. When I do, I send up a quick prayer for help.
- ❖ I see the person involved through eyes of mercy and grace, and I remind myself that none of us is perfect—certainly not myself.
- ❖ I remember the scriptural instruction not to take offense and I resolve to forgive the person/persons involved by an act of my will.

❖ I draw on the power of the indwelling Holy Spirit to drop the offense.

❖ I ask God to bless the person, touch them, meet their needs, and heal their hurts and wounds. And I pray for their prosperity of spirit, soul, and body.

❖ After the situation is over, I go to my heavenly Father with any wounds that have been inflicted upon me so his healing can flow over me. "Don't use foul or abusive language. Let everything you say be good and helpful, so that your words will be an encouragement to those who hear them. And do not bring sorrow to God's Holy Spirit by the way you live. Remember, he is the one who has identified you as his own, guaranteeing that you will be saved on the day of redemption. Get rid of all bitterness, rage, anger, harsh words, and slander, as well as all types of malicious behavior. Instead, be kind to each other, tenderhearted, forgiving one another, just as God through Christ has forgiven you" (Eph. 4:29–32 NLT).

Our God shall cause us to triumph in Christ Jesus (2 Cor. 2:14) as we choose to call on the power of the indwelling Spirit of God and let the offense find no lodging in our spirits. There may be recurring instances that will have to be dealt with openly with the person involved. It should always be done with love and gentleness, without anger or malice. Seek God's wisdom and guidance first.

Frances Frangipane states, "the destiny God has for man unfolds or dies at the junction of offense. How we handle offense is the key to our tomorrow."[2] Pastor Frances also stated, in a web writing no longer posted on his site, that it is wise to remember that "taking offense turns off the power of God in our lives." In addition, it makes us miserable.

It is a great victory when we begin to practice letting offenses go. It is like seeing a chain ready to wrap around us and we duck to avoid it. The same principle applies to our spirit when we do not allow an offense to take root. It becomes easier and easier to just "let it go." When we release a situation, God takes over and we see him move. We step out from between the other person and him by releasing our judgment. Doing so makes the opportunity for God to intervene. We experience a very satisfying peace, but it will not come until the initial temptation to take offense is dealt with. Little shadowy temptations may still dance around our minds, trying to stir up agitation. Just say "no" to them. How good it feels to walk free of garbage that others knowingly or unknowingly may try to dump on us.

Sensitive to Others

Just as I am learning to live free of offense, I try to be careful in my actions and speech so I do not offend others. I heard a story of a couple who were in a Sunday school class at church. The lady told me that several of the couples made lunch plans in front of them and never invited them to go. Another lady told of a situation where a woman walked up at church as she and a friend were talking. All three were friends. The lady greeted both as she approached and then said to one of the ladies in a very animated, excited voice, "Sally, we must have lunch together." She was completely oblivious to the fact that she was excluding one of the two.

We have to assess situations before speaking. One lady told me how hurtful it was upon telling someone she was getting a divorce (after years of abuse and seeking help) for them to immediately ask, "Have you been to a marriage counselor?" It was like fuel on a raging fire of pain.

Patricia spends a few moments every morning recalling the previous day to determine if she could have hurt someone by her speech or action. If something comes to her mind she determines to make the situation right even if she has to call the person involved. Recognizing her part in these situations is a vital part of the focus. Praying the "Serenity Prayer" is also part of her daily practice:

> God, grant me the serenity to accept the things I cannot change, courage to change the things I can, and the wisdom to know the difference.

She also prays, "Help me to set aside all of the things I think I know in order to have a new experience." In other words, Patricia does not want to be fenced in by thinking she is always right, knows it all, or has arrived. One of her mottoes is, "Be wrong/be happy. It is okay not to be perfect."

Suggested Prayer

Lord, help me to recognize when Satan is trying to get me into conflict with others. Grant me the maturity not to take the bait but to trust you to correct the wrongs sent in my direction. In the name of Jesus. Amen.

Reflection

1. How do you deal with feeling slighted, overlooked, or not appreciated?

2. Are you constantly trying to explain or justify your actions? Why do you feel that you need to do this?

3. Do old memories or slights still linger in your mind? What can you do about these? Would you like to be free in this part of your life? How can that happen?

Chapter 5

FREE TO FORGIVE

If we allow offenses to wrap around us the struggle to forgive can be very burdensome. Forgiving others, however, is not conditional for the one who has decided to follow Christ. God's instruction to his children does not include his making allowances for what others have done to us. Nowhere does Scripture say we can justify unforgiveness by the severity of the word or acts perpetuated against us. We are told to forgive so we may be forgiven. Pure and simple. That is not necessarily what we want to hear, but we are wise to remind ourselves of this truth.

Jesus' Words

"And whenever you stand praying, if you have anything against anyone, forgive him and let it drop (leave it, let it go), in order that your Father Who is in heaven may also forgive you your [own] failings and shortcomings and let them drop" (Mark 11:25 AMPLIFIED).

One paraphrase of this passage reads this way: "When you assume the posture of prayer, remember that it's not all asking. If you have anything against someone, forgive—only then will your heavenly Father be inclined to also wipe your slate clean of sins" (MESSAGE). Forgiveness is a commandment and not merely a suggestion.

Followers of Christ come face to face with the fact that our own forgiveness is directly linked to our willingness to forgive others. That is a very sobering thought. Moreover, unforgiveness clogs the channel of blessings that flow to us from our heavenly Father. Walking in unforgiveness gives Satan control in our lives and is one reason our prayers are not answered.

Jesus' Example

Jesus set a profound example of forgiveness as he hung on the cross. He had been beaten, his side pierced, with a crown of thorns crushed into his head. He experienced physical thirst, but more agonizing than that was his spiritual thirst as he cried, "'*Eli, Eli, lema sabachthani?*' which means 'My God, my God, why have you abandoned me?'" (Matt. 27:46 NLT). In the midst of his extreme agony he cried, "Father, forgive them, for they don't know what they are doing" (Luke 23:34 NLT).

Jesus wants to ignite in his followers the same response to others who have wronged us. He wants to turn us loose in a world where people will be amazed that we do not respond to the conflicts that beset us with "get even" values. "We are not called to be doormats but to let the love of Christ so manifest in our lives that people will recognize we are operating from another resource and they will be drawn to that resource through its display in our lives."[1]

Obedience

As a follower of Jesus we need to understand that forgiving others is a decision we choose to make. It is not an emotion. We choose not to give offense a place between ourselves and others. Nor do we save up reminders of another's weakness, fallibility, or inferior position to use against them.

Jane confided, "After being married for many years, I was one of the women whose husbands found someone else—a so-called friend of mine, no less. It is true she had lured him away, but he willingly followed. I was devastated. What had I done to deserve all of this heartache? Why God? Why?

"It seemed God had gone deaf to my pleas, and that he was ignoring my sorrow. I found it hard to forgive the ones who had inflicted so much hurt on me. Yet after a long, intense struggle, I was able to do just that, and I began praying for them. I discovered that forgiveness let me out of the prison of bitterness and hate. I addressed the layers of pain, and through struggle and prayer I was set free of unforgiveness."

Marge's marriage breakup was compounded by issues of sexual addiction on the part of her pastor husband. It was not just one woman, it was many! She shares: "It was supposed to be the storybook marriage I had dreamed of all my life. Instead, after a number of years and two children, I was standing over the stove making spaghetti for supper when he came in and proclaimed, 'I don't love you, I have never loved you, and I am tired of living a lie. I want out.'

"I grew up in a Christian home and made a decision for Christ at an early age. The man I married was a youth minister and together we had a wonderful, very successful ministry. I seemed to have left behind the low self-esteem that started when I was not selected for the cheerleading team in high school, even though I had performed excellently at the tryouts. After that, my self-worth was again attacked when a young man I was dating broke up with me—another rejection. I had noted tension was building in our marriage, but we were very busy with family and ministry. We sought counseling, at which time I discovered we were thirty-five thousand dollars in debt with nothing to show for it.

"The counselor clued me in that maybe my minister husband was involved in escort services, pornography, and prostitution. I was appalled. How could he accuse my husband of such a thing? As I drove home I had to pull the car over, because I was crying so hard I was unable to see the road. I screamed out. 'Lord are you there? Wake up! Please help me.' Immediately the thought came to me to look in the car's trunk. Did I get an eye full! There were XXX video tapes, pornography magazines, and two video tapes that were not labeled. I later discovered these tapes were of my husband in various hotel rooms—as well as our home—involved in sexual acts with other women.

"Hurt, betrayal, anger, and lonely feelings all overwhelmed me. The counselor advised me not to confront my husband until our next counseling session, which was not for another week. During this time I watched my husband give wonderful devotions at church and quote God's word from memory. The people thought he was wonderful. Again I struggled with low self-esteem. Did God really care for me and love me?

"During the confrontation at the counselor's office, my husband was calm, apologized, and promised to forsake this behavior. As the months went by it became clear he was a sex addict. He could not stop. I discovered he had struggled with this problem for years. We eventually left ministry and had to file for bankruptcy. I found a job outside the home. We lived under the same roof but separately for the next five years. During this time I went to the Word of God often to sustain me and help me work through much bitterness, loneliness, and unforgiveness. This intense work was the key for me being set free in my emotions. The Bible tells us in Matthew, 'If you forgive those who sin against you, your heavenly Father will forgive you. But if you refuse to forgive others, your Father will not forgive your sins' (6:14–15 NLT). Ouch! I wanted to tear that page out of my Bible. I discovered that forgiveness is a difficult process and usually does not happen all at once.

"The divorce became final and I had to watch as my husband drove up in a U-Haul® truck to take away furniture in preparation for living with someone else. The children had to be exposed to this change as they went to stay with them every other weekend. This too was a bitter pill to swallow. God provided furniture, gifts of money, and support through other people as he gave me the strength to continue in my job and raise our children.

"Then the toughest test came. My former husband was diagnosed with stage four colon cancer, which required major surgery and a long hospital stay due to complications. My now-adult daughter begged me to go with her every day to visit. God gave me the strength to do so. The patient in the next bed called me over and read the verse from

Isaiah 43:18–19, which declares, 'Forget the former things; do not dwell on the past, See I am doing a new thing!' (NIV). How did he know my situation? A higher being must have clued him in.

"Our children were now in high school and college and very busy with approaching finals. Someone had to take care of their father, because he no longer had a wife or girlfriend. God seemed to tap me on the shoulder and directed me to be the one to provide all the care required, including driving him to the doctor. This was a real test, but I passed it. I am happy to say he is now cancer-free.

"All of this was not without tremendous struggle, but the Lord brought me through it. I have been able to let go of the bitterness and unforgiveness. Of course, it wants to grip me again but I now know, 'Therefore, if the Son makes you free you shall be free indeed'" (John 8:36 NKJV). "I have learned to draw my self-esteem from the one who made me. I know that my strength comes from him as I obey his Word."

Marge is to be greatly admired for coming through this situation in victory.

Forgiving Self

It was a real revelation for me to discover that sometimes we have problems forgiving because we have not really owned up to our part in a hurtful situation and forgiven ourselves. I believe this is especially true in family issues. Jane confided that she had come to realize why she had not let go of lingering memories involving unwise decisions her children made as young adults. It was because she had not forgiven herself for the immature way she had reacted. Once she looked at the issues and asked the Lord to forgive her for her part, then she was able to leave it behind her. Part of the secret to forgiving ourselves is simply to acknowledge that we are not perfect and that we do not always make perfect, rational decisions.

Katie shares: "In 1966, in my second year of nursing school, I was following the crowd, partying, and 'looking for love in all the wrong places.' Weekend social events were filled with alcohol and lost inhibitions. Instead of love and acceptance, I found myself pregnant and rejected. I dropped out of school and out of sight. The following year I gave birth to a beautiful baby girl. I could not take my eyes off of her in the delivery room. She was innocent, with dark eyes, and searching her new world in wonderment.

"Later that day I was wheeled past the nursery and, with a broken heart and tears clouding my vision, I said good-bye to my precious baby girl. I did not accept the option a few days later to hold her, as I knew that if I held her I would not be able to let her go. I had nothing to offer her. I left a piece of my heart behind, signed adoption papers, and moved on with my life. I finished nursing school, got married, gave my wounded heart to Jesus, and had two more beautiful daughters, but I never forgot my firstborn. Scripture asks in Isaiah 49:15, 'Can a mother forget her nursing child? Can she feel no love for the child she has borne?' (NLT). The answer is a resounding NEVER! Was my daughter happy? Was she healthy? What did she look like? Where does she live? Will I ever be able to tell her I've always loved her? Does she know about her birth mother and does she hate me?

"In the late 1970s and 1980s, with the death of my dad and some problems in my marriage, my world started to crumble. Although I had asked Jesus to be my Savior, there was still something missing. I felt so desolate. I found myself reading Jeremiah 29:11–13, 'For I know the plans I have for you, says the Lord. They are plans for good and not for disaster, to give you a future and a hope. In those days when you pray, I will listen. If you look for me in earnest, you will find me when you seek me' (NLT). I began praying and seeking Jesus with all of my heart. The more desperate my circumstances, the more I cried out.

"One particularly painful day in the summer of 1982 I took a walk in the woods to reflect on my life. I felt compelled to cry out to God for the child I'd left behind. 'Father, I don't know where she is but you do, and I pray you will make her yours and then I know she will be okay.' Even if a mother could forget her newborn child, God would not. Even if my child thought that her birth mother had rejected and forgotten her, she needed to know that God would never do that and that she could find her security in him.

"In 1988 I decided to join ALMA, a reunion registry that matches people who are searching for each other. Ten years later in silence I did not renew my membership and released my child completely to the Lord with full assurance that if it was meant to be, God would reunite us in his time.

"One year later I receive an e-mail from my daughter with 'Hello—thank you for my life' in the subject line. Within two weeks my two daughters and I went to Atlanta to meet Nancie and her family. I finally got to hold my grown-up baby! I saw the fulfillment of Romans 8:28, 'And we know that in all things God works for the good of those who love him, who have been called according to his purpose' (NIV). He has taken my repentant sin and turned it into a blessing.

"Today I have the privilege of serving God by doing ultrasounds in my local Assurance Pregnancy Center, and regularly encourage our clients to look at the big picture. What seems like an impossible situation can turn into a blessing down the road. It doesn't take a crisis pregnancy to experience a miracle in your life; sometimes it just takes a crisis. Every crisis is an opportunity for God to show up. I'm convinced God's favorite word is impossible—because with God, all things are possible!"

"It is possible to have your sins blotted out of God's book, but not out of your conscience."[2] When we allow this festering within ourselves, it is as if we are refusing God's grace. Scripture gives four promises of God's dealings with confessed sin.

1. He remembers them no more. "I—yes, I alone—will blot out your sins for my own sake and will never think of them again" (Isa. 43:25 NLT).
2. He removes them as far as the east is from the west. "He has removed our sins as far from us as the east is from the west" (Ps. 103:12 NLT).
3. He hurls our iniquities into the depths of the sea. "Once again you will have compassion on us. You will trample our sins under your feet and throw them into the depths of the ocean!" (Mic. 7:19 NLT).

4. He puts them behind his back. "In your love you kept me from the pit of destruction; you have put all my sins behind your back" (Isa. 38:17 NIV).

If God himself is so emphatic about pardoning, forgiving, and forgetting sin, why should we, mere human beings, refuse to accept his gracious forgiveness?

Practical Steps

Once we choose to walk in God's commandment to forgive and then allow his love to flow out of us to others, we should ask God to bring our emotions in line. We can learn to ignore any "temper fits" coming out of our feelings. We can choose to yield to the power of the Holy Spirit who lives within those who have experienced his transformation.

Human love is inadequate. It always seems to fall short at some point! We may find we need to ask the heavenly Father to fill our heart with his love for specific people. With this infilling we start growing into the 1 Corinthians 13:4–7 definition of love, "Love is patient and kind. Love is not jealous or boastful or proud or rude. Love does not demand its own way. Love is not irritable, and it keeps no record of when it has been wronged. It is never glad about injustice but rejoices whenever the truth wins out. Love never gives up, never loses faith, is always hopeful, and endures through every circumstance" (Living translation). This growth begins to develop as we allow the Holy Spirit more expression through us.

At this point there is a vital step that I missed for many years. I would push the offense I was dealing with away and not acknowledge it. This action was rooted in the misconception that good and mature people would not let this type of situation bother them. Thus I would push the accompanying pain away. It would get buried. Another way of dealing with this situation was to spew negative remarks over anyone near me about the offense, thus degrading and slandering the other person involved.

Expose the Hurt and Pain to the Great Physician

Own the pain involved. It is very important to bring our hurt and pain to the Lord in prayer. Don't just say, "I forgive them," in a casual manner, but expose all of the hurt and pain to Jesus. Lay all of the pain and hurt before him in prayer so the root of the problem is pulled out rather than just chopped off. Otherwise, it will grow right back. When this step is missed, we are not able to work out complete forgiveness, because all of our pain has not been exposed.

The following steps have helped me:

1. Confess any specific wrongdoing or bad attitude and ask for forgiveness. Do not generalize by saying, "If I have done anything to provoke or promote this …" Own up to your part in the situation.
2. Decide to extend forgiveness to the person involved, and release them from what they have done. Be specific.
3. Go to the person for the purpose of reconciliation. "[If] you suddenly remember that someone has something against you, leave your sacrifice there at the altar. Go and be reconciled to that person" (Matt. 5:23–24 NLT).
4. Perform a random act of kindness for the person. This marks the decision to forgive and puts Satan on notice that we are living out the commandment to forgive. It is important to have a date or action to point to when the enemy tries to get us to pick up the offense again.

Satan will always try to get us to take our eyes off of Jesus and the victory we have experienced. It is wise to be alert to this and refuse it in the name of the Lord Jesus Christ through the power of the Holy Spirit living within those who have allowed him to transform their lives.

The healing process begins the moment the choice is made to release the grip of an unforgiving spirit. It is a process and can be quite a struggle.

Many people think blame has to be established before we can forgive, but that is a deception. We can be sorry a relationship has been broken, and we can express that sorrow without assigning blame. Satan has been out to divide us since the beginning of time. We must recognize this to walk in victory in our relationships. I mentioned earlier that Satan can "shade" what we hear and cause us to misinterpret things that were said. Our hearing is filtered through past emotions, hurts, and expectations. Satan also wants to rob us of our joy and peace. He wants to defeat us in our living out the principles that bring us freedom. He does not want us to be free of the chains of unforgiveness.

It helps to remind ourselves that we are all involved in the ongoing process of becoming more spiritually mature. We must have mercy for the areas of immaturity in others, just as we need them to extend mercy to us in our shortcomings. "Understand (this) my beloved brethren. Let every man be quick to hear (a ready listener), slow to speak, slow to take offense and to get angry" (James 1:19 AMPLIFIED). As we learn to live more and more by this scripture, offense will come less often, thus requiring a decreasing need to forgive. The temptation to take offense will not find fertile soil in our spirits. "Most important of all, continue to show deep love for each other, for love covers a multitude of sins" (1 Pet. 4:8 NLT).

Some Insights about Forgiveness

Forgiveness is *not* overlooking

Forgiveness is *not* a feeling

Forgiveness is *not* pretending I was not hurt

Forgiveness is *not* saying what the other person did was not so bad

Forgiveness is *not* relieving others of their responsibility

Forgiveness does *not* mean that I have to have a close friendship or establish a trust relationship with the person involved

Forgiveness *is* transferring the accountability of their actions over to God so that he can deal with them

Freedom Found in Forgiving

Forgiveness is a decision we make to obey God and to walk free from offense with all others. We decide that we will not allow someone else's actions or attitudes to dictate our responses towards them. Forgiveness is getting our own hearts right before our heavenly Father. And it is guarding against a bitter root finding a place to grow in our spirit.

> Try to live in peace with everyone, and seek to live a clean and holy life, for those who are not holy will not see the Lord. Look after each other so that none of you will miss out on the special favor of God. Watch out that no bitter root of unbelief rises up among you, for whenever it springs up, many are corrupted by its poison.
> —Hebrews 12:14–15 NLT

When we forgive others we release God to do his restoring work with the other person involved. We step from between God and the person. Forgiveness frees God to act on our behalf. We put the situation in God's hands, and when we forgive in this way, we feel the release of a heavy burden, which brings us peace.

Any person or memory that unsettles us has the potential for unforgiveness. If we want to avoid a person this may signal wounds not dealt with. Face this and take it to God in prayer. Past wounds will surface, tempting us to take them up again. The Bible says, "Grow up. You're kingdom subjects. Now live like it. Live generously and graciously towards others, the way God lives towards you" (Matt. 5:48 MESSAGE). "But, I say love your enemies. Pray for those who persecute you. In that way you will be acting as true children of your Father in heaven" (Matt. 5:44 NLT). "You must be compassionate, just as your Father is compassionate" (Luke 6:36 NLT).

Unforgiveness has two relatives named *bitterness* and *resentment*. Any person or memory that makes our blood pressure rise indicates there is something in the past that is not resolved. Bitterness is deadly spiritually, emotionally, and physically.

When we choose the position of forgiveness, this puts our emotional health and destiny in God's hands rather than giving the person involved power over us. Forgiveness says, "No, in the name of Jesus, I am going to rise above this and not let another person's problem become my problem." The decision is made not to respond back in anger. A wrong reaction on our part is just as bad as the initial wrong action against us.

Forgiveness will free the other person involved from the bondage our bitterness or resentment would place on them. "Forgiveness transforms lives, causing the windows of heaven to open. It fills our cup of spiritual blessing to the brim, with abundant peace, joy, and rest in the Holy Ghost."[3] Forgiveness will free us.

Wisdom

We can ask God to direct us as to as whether we need to go to the person we have forgiven. Sometimes doing this can cause great harm, or sometimes it is not possible due to death or distance. If we do go to the person it is important to ask them, "Will you forgive me?" Get an answer. If they say they will forgive you, rejoice. If they say they will not, or if they refuse to answer (which means no), then the spiritual responsibility goes over to them. Matthew 5:23–24 speaks of the action to take if you know someone else has something against you. "[If] you suddenly remember that someone has something against you, leave your sacrifice there at the altar. Go and be reconciled to that person" (NLT). The heart of the matter is to talk it out with God, to follow the steps outlined for forgiving, and then remember not to nurse the offense. Don't rehearse it, let it go!

The offense may have been against us, in which case we may still seek resolution. Walk as a free person having freed the other person by your forgiveness, or by doing all in your power to seek forgiveness from them for your failures against them. "Forgiveness is not total forgiveness until we bless our enemies and pray for them to be blessed. Forgiving them is a major step; totally forgiving them has fully been achieved when we set God free to bless them."[4] A step further is for us to be willing to be an unrestricted channel for God's blessings to flow through us to that person.

If we are not able to break free from the pain incurred from the tongue or action of others, we can talk to a counselor, a mature Christian, or a pastor.

Forgiving Yourself

Many of us have never thought to apply the same act of forgiveness to ourselves as Scripture clearly indicates we are to extend to others.

We have all done things we regret. Some of us repent over and over but continue to be weighted down by the burden of remembrance. Memories and self-accusations bombard us. We know in our minds that we are forgiven once we confess. We know the truth of 1 John 1:9, "But if we confess our sins to him, he is faithful and just to forgive us and to cleanse us from every wrong" (NLT). But while we may know this truth, we may not receive it as related to our own sins of willful disobedience to a commandment of God.

We may have hurt, slandered, and rejected others, and committed sins of various types. Some acts may have been illegal. Other acts, while not illegal, were outside of God's standards set forth in Scripture. In any event, we have all fallen short. "For everyone has sinned; we all fall short of God's glorious standard" (Rom. 3:23 NLT).

We read various accounts in the Bible of Jesus encountering sinners. It is interesting to note in Luke's gospel Jesus' comments spoken in regard to a former prostitute. He made the point that those who are forgiven of the greatest debt will also have the greatest love for him.

> "But neither of them could repay him, so he kindly forgave them both, canceling their debts. Who do you suppose loved him more after that?" Simon answered, "I suppose the one for whom he canceled the larger debt." "That's right," Jesus said. Then he turned to the woman and said to Simon, "Look at this woman kneeling here. When I entered your home, you didn't offer me water to wash the dust from my feet, but she has washed them with her tears and wiped them with her hair. You didn't greet me with a kiss, but from the time I first came in, she has not stopped kissing my feet. You neglected the courtesy of olive oil to anoint my head, but she has anointed my feet with rare perfume. I tell you, her sins—and they are many—have been forgiven, so she has shown me much love. But a person who is forgiven little shows only little love." Then Jesus said to the woman, "Your sins are forgiven."
>
> —Luke 7:42–48 NLT

After we take our shame and guilt to Christ in initial surrender, we become a new creation. Our sins are washed away and they are remembered no more. We walk in newness of life—a new creation born of God's Holy Spirit. The old has gone, the new has come. Is this not awesome?

We must apply the same mercy and grace in forgiving ourselves as we are commanded to extend to others. No sin is too big or terrible for God's forgiveness, so why should we hold onto it? The Christian's archenemy, Satan, will use every means to get us to continue to focus on our mistakes, shortcomings, and errors. He will attempt to make us feel totally unworthy, defeated, and without hope in our personal struggles to follow Jesus Christ and his teachings.

Jesus offered his life through his blood sacrifice on the cross not only to transform us as we first make the decision to follow him, but to completely set us free. He provides the power to overcome temptation and sin on a day-to-day basis. Step up, claim, and use that power.

We take the acts we continue to commit to God in prayer and ask for forgiveness. Once we confess these acts, and in some cases make restitution, then they are gone. He remembers them no more and does not hold them against us. We do not have to continue focusing on them or be plagued by thoughts of the acts. Remind Satan aloud that they are dealt with by quoting the scripture in 1 John 1:9, "But if we confess our sins to him, he is faithful and just to forgive us our sins and to cleanse us from all wickedness" (NLT). This is following the pattern Jesus gave as he himself quoted Scripture to Satan during his forty-day wilderness experience: "The Scriptures say, … the Scriptures say, … the Scriptures also say …" (Luke 4:1–3).

Many things from our past may leave guilty scars on our hearts. The way out of this is through confession, asking for forgiveness, and then receiving the heavenly Father's gracious provision. A very interesting story is told by Grant Mullens, a Canadian mental health physician, concerning a lady with severe lingering back pain. The pain had resulted from an automobile accident. The driver of the other car, who had plowed into her vehicle, was clearly at fault. The accident had occurred sometime prior to the meeting where the injured lady joined a healing line to request prayer.

Upon hearing the origin of the problem Dr. Mullens asked if she had forgiven the person who was responsible for the accident. This had not occurred to her. She readily agreed that she had not, and Dr. Mullens led her in a prayer of forgiveness. Following this she was completely relieved of the back problem. It is very interesting that she did not knowingly hold resentment, but in some mysterious way healing was released after she forgave. Her prayer of forgiveness was not just rote words. She forgave the person on a deep level.[5]

We do know there is a connection between the three parts of a person, which are: body, soul (mind, will, emotions), and spirit. What affects one affects the other. Discord and disorder in one area cross over in some unknown way and often cause problems in the other as the parts of our personhood cannot be isolated from each other.

Olivia's story is an example of this. She was the picture of peace and composure as she sat across the room from me in a prayer gathering. Later she shared her story. I discovered it had taken years to work through the pain of her childhood and to reach this tranquil state.

Olivia's mother was physically and verbally abusive, slapping her and beating on her for the slightest childish behavior. Sometimes it was because Olivia did not meet her unreasonable, perfectionist expectations. The child was almost afraid to move for fear she would bring her mother's wrath and heavy hair brush or switch down on her. She never had any words of affection or affirmation or praise. There was just constant correction and criticism.

As an adult Olivia sought help for the root of her problems, which manifested as emotional turmoil, depression, nightmares, and recurring bouts of weight gain (she once ballooned to 286 pounds). She was in a see-saw cycle, losing weight only to regain it. She was trying to hide the real Olivia and cover up all of the pain.

After seeking answers with a Christian counselor, Olivia dreamed that her father had sexually abused her one time at about age three. She never confronted him, but she did write him a letter telling him she forgave him for anything he had done, not naming to what she was referring. He wrote back that it was gracious of her to forgive him. When he didn't even ask for what, she felt the violation was confirmed.

Olivia came to faith in Jesus Christ at the age of eight years, so she had a resource to turn to when she began facing the trauma in her life as a young adult. Initially, the husband she married was critical and harsh, making her feel she had married someone who treated her verbally like her mother. Following a life-changing encounter with Jesus Christ, he became a wonderful support as she struggled to throw off the chains of the years of abuse. After much prayer, counseling, anxiety medication, and the support of her loving husband, Olivia has reached a position of victory and is at her goal weight after having lost 142 pounds.

At one point her mother, who is now deceased, confessed that she had not been a very good mother. They became very close in her mother's later years. Olivia feels her problems were rooted in the abuse that was heaped upon her over the years. At one time a voice within her prompted her to "just get it over with." But the loving voice of Jesus responded with, "I don't want you to do this."

When I visited Olivia in her home I saw a very composed, peaceful, middle-aged woman. She excels in singing, scrapbooking, card making, and beautiful watercolor and oil painting. She is a loving mother and grandmother to her two adult sons, their wives and children. She feels the victory was always there, she just had to walk it out.

There are a number of avenues to wholeness which Olivia used. They included antidepressant and anxiety medication, light lamp therapy (a special light individuals have found helpful to sit under for specific periods in the winter months when exposure to sunshine is limited), and counseling, as well as prayers by those experienced in praying. Olivia now spends a lot of time feeding her spirit with prayer and Scripture reading as well as speaking aloud specific Scriptural promises. The result is she does not need to feed her body as much. She walks in the freedom that Jesus promises, "If the Son sets you free, you will be free indeed" (John 8:36 NIV).

Suggested Prayer

Lord, help me to remember the price you paid so I could be forgiven for my sins. In obedience to your words telling me to forgive, I want to extend forgiveness to those who have hurt me. I do not want to block your blessings by holding on to grudges, resentments, and hostility. I want to roll all of those challenges over onto you and have you decide on any action to be taken. Thank you for the freedom you made available for me to choose to walk in forgiveness. Amen.

Reflection

1. Are there people who hurt you deeply? How have they done this?

2. What steps have you taken to forgive them?

3. Why is it true that your own forgiveness hinges on you forgiving others?

4. Are you willing to forgive and turn the situation over to God? What is the best way to do that?

5. Will you make a list of those you need to forgive and work through it?

Chapter 6

THE POWER OF WORDS

Most of the words spoken since the creation of the world have been forgotten. Some words, however, are remembered for years. These are the words that build up and affirm others, and the words that wound. One woman recounted how being called "dumb as a door knob" by a parent had oppressed her for fifty years. She then discovered how to be free as she refused to let those words continue echoing in her head. How did she do this? She examined the statement spoken into her spirit and determined it was not true. It had been a "word curse" over her life that held her captive for years and years. She forgave the parent who harmed her with these words, and now she is free of the chain that had bound her for so long.

Many words of inspiration live on in print. They may take on life even years after they were written, as a reader's mind is illuminated by the ideas presented. Proverbs 18:21 states, "The tongue can bring death or life; those who love to talk will reap the consequences" (NLT). It is sobering to read in Matthew's gospel, "I tell you this, you must give an account on judgment day for every idle word you speak. The words you say will either acquit you or condemn you" (12:36–37 NLT).

The Tongue

The third chapter of the book of James gives a powerful word picture of controlling the tongue:

> Dear brothers and sisters, not many of you should become teachers in the church, for we who teach will be judged more strictly. Indeed, we all make many mistakes. For if we could control our tongues, we would be perfect and could also control ourselves in every other way. We can make a large horse go wherever we want by means of a small bit in its mouth. And a small rudder makes a huge ship turn wherever the pilot chooses to go, even though the winds are strong. In the same way, the tongue is a small thing that makes grand speeches. But a tiny spark can set a great forest on fire. And the tongue is a flame of fire. It is a whole world of wickedness, corrupting your entire body. It can set your whole life on fire, for it is set on fire by hell itself. People can tame all kinds of animals, birds, reptiles, and fish, but no one can tame the tongue. It is restless and evil, full of deadly poison. Sometimes it praises our Lord and Father, and sometimes it curses those who have been made in the image of God. And so blessing and cursing come pouring out of the same mouth. Surely, my brothers and sisters, this is not right! Does a spring of water bubble out with both fresh water and bitter water? Does a fig tree produce olives, or a grapevine produce figs? No, and you can't draw fresh water from a salty spring.
>
> —James 3:1–12 NLT

We are told that mastering control of the tongue is the secret to the control of the self in every other way. The tongue is compared to a tiny spark that sets a great forest on fire and causes a blazing flame of destruction. It is wise to remember spoken words cannot be retracted. A fire can be extinguished, but the charred remains are left.

Atmosphere

Ras Robinson (www.fullnessonline.org) stated in his daily inspirational e-mail, dated May 17, 2005, that, "The very atmosphere around you is colored and affected by the words you speak. Consider your words as your treasure and treat them as precious gold and jewels."

Another way to look at words is that they are like boomerangs. Throw them out and they come back, sometimes to hit us and cause us great trouble. It is difficult to learn to control the words we speak but with attention and practice it can be mastered. We also need to learn to determine how true the words are that others speak to us and about us. This is a huge step towards being free. I am learning to guard the words I speak both to myself (self-talk) and to others. Robinson also wrote that, "Words can create a firestorm of enemy activity designed to destroy unity and create strife."

As we learn to be more secure in our uniqueness we have less need to correct, set others straight, or allow anger to flare up. I have found it wise to check my motives when speaking. Even in casual conversations at social gatherings, I have discovered underlying fragments of desires to impress others.

Our prayer as Christians can be, "Take control of what I say, O Lord, and guard my lips" (Ps. 141:3 NLT). John F. Stephens states, "The secret to the victorious Christian life is in the mouth."[1]

Regard For Others/Self

We learn to treat others with kindness and to give thought before we speak hastily. The Bible gives clear instructions about what we need to do when we find a fellow believer who is in sin:

> If another believer sins against you, go privately and point out the offense. If the other person listens and confesses it, you have won that person back. But if you are unsuccessful, take one or two others with you and go back again, so that everything you say may be confirmed by two or three witnesses. If the person still refuses to listen, take your case to the church. Then if he or she won't accept the church's decision, treat that person as a pagan or a corrupt tax collector.
> —Matthew 18:15–17 NLT

Many of us have a habit of speaking unkind words about ourselves. It is well to note that it is not conceited to recognize our strengths and reinforce those in our thinking and speaking. If we constantly "put ourselves down" by speaking rejection, defeat, or disaster of varying degrees, these very things then rush in to fill up the atmosphere around us. Our negative words provide a way for the enemy, Satan, to reinforce our words and use them against us. We eventually become what we speak. In some mysterious way our words create a vacuum on the inside of us and the very things we have spoken eventually come and take up habitation. Our words register on our spirits and control us, eventually becoming a self-fulfilling prophecy.

There are cultures where arrows are stuck into cloth dolls as a way of cursing the ones represented by the dolls. When we speak against ourselves, it is like stabbing the creation God made as he formed us in our mother's womb. When we turn and attack ourselves with our own words, essentially we are stabbing ourselves. According to E.W. Kenyon, "Every time you confess disease and weakness and failure, you magnify the adversary above the Father, and you destroy your own confidence in the Word. Do not magnify Satan above the Father!"[2]

Kenyon goes on to state that, "Our confession imprisons us. The right kind of confession will set us free. It is not only our thinking; it is our words, our conversation that builds power or weakness in us."[3]

We can learn to evaluate what others say to us and about us. This helps us not to accept untrue statements into our inner being. We do not have to become angry or retaliate. We just examine what is said. If it is not true, we do not let the words penetrate our spirit and disrupt our peace. The temptation is always present to set others straight, but it is freeing to just let it go. As I have faced these situations over and over I am learning about true freedom and have grown in the discipline of refusing to believe things about myself that are not true.

Jan's story demonstrates how powerful words can be in helping us identify and remove the chains that bind us. She wanted to stand up and say, "That's me," when she heard her minister give a description of generalized anxiety disorder. Anxiety had ruled Jan's life since childhood. When they talked about fire safety at school she immediately worried that her house would catch on fire. She came home and forced her family to practice their escape route. Information about possible tornados terrified her.

THE POWER OF WORDS

For a time Jan could talk herself out of a negative thought and move on with life. Then the anxiety began intensifying and leading to periods of depression. She would dwell on the bad stuff for several hours, sometimes for days.

Jan lived with a feeling of impending doom much of the time. The obsessive, anxiety-driven thoughts soon developed into thoughts of catastrophe and brought on panic attacks. The crisis came when Jan's child was born. At one point she could not get out of bed. She had daily panic attacks, constant sadness, paralyzing fear and anxiety, suicidal thoughts, and was apathetic about life. Fortunately Jan's husband and friends stood by her during this post-partum depression. She maintained an open dialogue with God during her long journey to recovery. She knew he was there to help her. She had entrusted her life to him as a child.

One day she was talking to a friend about her problems. The friend then drew a picture for Jan of a tree with several branches and a huge, thick, tangled root. On each branch she wrote an "issue" that they had talked about. Then she said, "This tree is a picture of what is going on in your soul. These branches represent the issues you are struggling with. You may resolve them one by one, but another branch or issue will grow back in its place. You have to find the root that is the source of all these little issues. You need to ask God to show you what the root is. Once you discover that, ask him to dig it up and plant a new tree in your heart."

Jan was thinking, "This is crazy. I don't have a root. I'm a good woman. I'm a minister's wife, and I've been a Christian for a long time. I just have a few minor issues." But the feeling persisted that what her friend had told her was the truth. When Jan sat down and had a long intense talk with God, she discovered that control was at the root of her issues. She prayed and asked God to take the root of control from her. At that moment she could physically feel the root untangling from around her until she was at peace.

Then God spoke to Jan. This was not a quiet still voice, but a voice that made her turn around because she thought someone was standing right behind her. He said, "Jan, you are free from all of it. You've surrendered all of it to me. It's gone. Washed clean. White as snow. Forever."

After sitting in stillness, shock, amazement, and peace for a long time, God revealed to Jan that the new tree planted in her heart was surrender. At first she thought this would make her weak and powerless, but then she considered what her previous life had looked like with all of the fear, worry, and anxiety. She recalled the scripture verse which says, "For God did not give us a spirit of timidity, but a spirit of power, of love and of self-discipline" (2 Tim. 1:7 NIV). Jan has learned to believe the truth of God's Word, despite what her feelings may try to dictate to her. The words spoken to her in love helped her get to the problem that had kept her bound.

Eternal Word

We have addressed what is in the realm of human words, but now we will consider the Word that is eternal and stands firm in heaven (Psalm 119:89). That Word is a "forever" Word. It is "my word that goes out from my mouth: It will not return to me empty but will accomplish what I desire and achieve the purpose for which I sent it" (Isa. 55:11 NIV). That Word is the Word of God. There is a myriad of promises contained within the pages of the Bible for the follower of Jesus Christ, and it is good to keep some of these at hand and declare them aloud.

Some Examples that Encourage

"The Lord is my fortress, protecting me from danger, so why should I tremble?"

—Psalm 27:1 NLT

"I can do everything through Christ, who gives me strength."

—Philippians 4:13 NLT

"For who has known the mind of the Lord that he may instruct him? But we have the mind of Christ."

—1 Corinthians 2:16 NIV

"No weapon forged against you will prevail, and you will refute every tongue that accuses you."

—Isaiah 54:17 NIV

"[He] forgives all your sins and heals all your diseases."

—Psalm 103:3 NIV

"He sent out his word and healed them, snatching them from the door of death."

—Psalm 107:20 NLT

"My God will meet all your needs according to his glorious riches in Christ Jesus."

—Philippians 4:19 NIV

"I will never leave you nor forsake you."

—Hebrews 13:5 NKJV

"All things work together for good to those who love God, to those who are the called according to His purpose."

—Romans 8:28 NKJV

"We are more than conquerors through him who loved us."

—Romans 8:37 NIV

"Confessing is confirming the Word of God. It is a confession of my confidence in what God has spoken."[4]

Persistence in Speaking the Word

"My son-in-law, John, was calling from halfway across the country when he had me paged at the airport. 'The baby is coming. I am taking Jane to the hospital now. You will have to take a taxi from the airport to the hospital,' John exclaimed.

"This was the young man who had married my daughter just a few short years before. On the eve of their wedding at the rehearsal dinner, I proposed a toast and presented my daughter with a lovely little apron and scissors with which to cut the apron strings. We were very close.

"Upon graduation from college she had given up her plans to find a job with her friends in New York or Washington, D.C., and came home to live with me. My unexpected divorce had stolen her dreams.

She laid down her own desires to help me through the difficult months that lay ahead. She lived with me for four years until her marriage, and then I was the one who had to cut the apron strings.

"After graduate school her husband took her to the Northwest. He prefaced the move with a promise that he would bring her home in two years if she felt too far away. Although the distance was great, it was a wonderful experience for them. Their move to Texas three years later, however, was not.

"I hung up the phone and boarded the plane. All of our plans to be together for the birth of the baby had vanished. Traveling to a city where I had never been, there would be no one to meet me at the airport. My daughter was giving birth while I was still trying to get there. I traveled for what seemed like hours. I finally arrived and rushed to the delivery room. There was a sigh of relief from two nurses as I entered the room. 'Your mother is here!'

"Baby Elizabeth was born that evening. What a joy it was to hold and pray over this baby girl in the first few minutes of her life. Now it was time for my son-in-law to bring these girls home.

"Although Jane gave a two year commitment to living in Texas, there was never a time when they were not praying about a move home. We experienced every emotion as we watched the commitment mark come and go. I found myself again at the same hospital praying over another baby girl, Margaret, in the first few minutes of her brand-new life. Now with two little babies, the distance between us was just too great. We praised and thanked God for where she was and we tried to accept it. Then we started all over again. The door did not open for them to move home, and we were beginning to lose hope.

"On January 15, 2003 God gave me a scripture: 'Lift up your eyes and look about you: All assemble and come to you; your sons come from afar, and your daughters are carried on the arm. Then you will look and be radiant, your heart will throb and swell with joy' (Isa. 60:4–5 NIV). I immediately saw my son-in-law coming home with my daughter and their children on his arm. I knew now that the Lord was bringing them home. It was just a matter of time. I prayed the scripture God had given me. I would have to hold steady, believe I had received what I prayed, and then actively look for their return.

"Weeks and months went by and God gave me another scripture on which to stand in faith. It was from the Old Testament book of Jeremiah, which declares, 'There is hope in your future, says the Lord, that your children shall come back to their own border' (31:17 NKJV). With this additional scripture I was really armed with faith. With these two words from God, there was no doubt that my daughter and her family would be returning.

"In March 2005, my son-in-law was offered a position with his company that would allow him to move home. A huge battle ensued as one department had to release him to another. Everyone wanted to keep him in Texas. But God had spoken! They were coming home! After days of complications God spoke to my heart and said to speak the Word over the situation that Moses spoke to Pharaoh—'Let my people go!' I began confessing this over my son-in-law and those who stood in his way. I called my daughter to agree in prayer. God had just given her the same message. Wow! She had spent five long years in Texas, but the end was in sight.

"The next month, at Easter, my children came to visit and bought a wonderful home right around the corner. Several months later they moved in. I saw the fulfillment of a dream God had given me some years prior where I was walking down the sidewalk, turned the corner, and there was little Elizabeth running straight into my arms! I am radiant, my heart swells with joy. Declaring the Word is powerful. Persistence yields answers."

Feeding Faith Versus Fear

There is a natural atmosphere as well as a spiritual atmosphere surrounding us. Our words are like "nourishment" to feed and enlarge what we are speaking into. Our words indicate whether we are moving in faith or fear. There is space for faith words as well as space for words of fear. Faith activates God's power and fear feeds into Satan's power. We need to line up our confessions with God's Word from Scripture. Speaking into the fear atmosphere gives Satan entrance into our situations.

What comes out of our mouths will control our future. It is the spiritual principle of sowing and reaping. The apostle Paul put it this way: "Do not be deceived: God cannot be mocked. A man reaps what he sows" (Gal. 6:7 NIV). It works for non-Christians as well as Christians. Each time we sow words of fear, we are feeding the fear and allowing it to grow stronger. The same is true of faith-filled words for "fear activates Satan as faith activates God."[5]

Continuing to speak words of defeat, failure, and sickness gives them power over us. Repetition reinforces them as our speaking expresses faith in what we say. Scripture tells us, "you have been trapped by what you said, ensnared by the words of your mouth" (Prov. 6:2 NIV). This is not the same as the "positive thinking" concept so widely taught for many years. The most positive thinking and speaking we can do is to speak aloud Scripture pertaining to the situation we face. Our heavenly Father loves to hear his words coming back to him from the mouths of his children. Compare this to the delight of earthly parents as they hear the concepts they have taught their children being spoken out of their own children's mouths. Often it is spoken as if it were the child's own idea. Following this the parent knows the child "got it." Likewise, our heavenly Father delights in knowing his children get it—they have studied his Word and have allowed it to be engrafted on their hearts.

Seeking out specific scriptures related to our circumstances and speaking them aloud helps us learn to speak God's words back to him and move from hope to faith. "Faith comes from hearing, that is, hearing the Good News about Christ" (Rom. 10:17 NLT). Speaking Scripture back to God feeds the faith atmosphere around us and not the fear atmosphere.

Power of the Indwelling Word

Jesus said, "If you remain in me and my words remain in you, ask whatever you wish, and it will be given you" (John 15:7 NIV). If we stay joined to Christ and his words remain in us and we remain in him, the Bible says we can ask any request and it will be granted. Needless to say, if we are abiding in him we will not be asking for inappropriate things which would be clearly outside of God's will. Rather, we will be guided by the indwelling Holy Spirit as well as what God reveals to us through the Scripture we seek out for the situations we are facing. We search out a firm foundation of specific scriptures and offer them back to the

Father in a spirit of praise, worship, and thanksgiving. Then any darkness and defeat surrounding us will start to recede. God's words spoken out of our mouths build us up in our inner beings as we hear them.

In some cases we have either not been taught or not been taught correctly about this. We must learn to think according to God's Word, and not according to how we were trained when those words do not line up with Scripture. We should not try to bring Scripture down to our experiences but rather to bring our experience up to the level of Scripture. The acid test is not what I think, not what others think, but what does God declare?

When God hears his Word he is obligated to perform it. We are told his Word will not return void but will accomplish that for which he sent it: "My word that goes out from my mouth: It will not return to me empty, but will accomplish what I desire and achieve the purpose for which I sent it" (Isa. 55:11 NIV).

Believer/Confessing

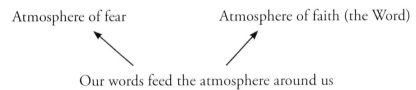

Atmosphere of fear   Atmosphere of faith (the Word)

Our words feed the atmosphere around us

Which will you feed? An atmosphere of fear, or one of faith in the Word of God? Which will you agree with? Will you release faith in God or release faith in the Enemy by speaking fearful thoughts?

Words of Salvation

God places great emphasis on confessing (speaking) to receive salvation. Paul writes that, "If you confess with your mouth that Jesus is Lord and believe in your heart that God raised him from the dead, you will be saved. For it is by believing in your heart that you are made right with God, and it is by confessing with your mouth that you are saved" (Rom. 10:9–10 NLT).

Salvation includes more than just giving us entrance into heaven when we die. According to Isaiah 53:4–6, Jesus carried our weakness, our sorrows, our sins, and provided healing as well as peace: "Yet it was our weaknesses he carried; it was our sorrows that weighed him down. And we thought his troubles were a punishment from God, a punishment for his own sins! But he was pierced for our rebellion, crushed for our sins. He was beaten so we could be whole. He was whipped so we could be healed. All of us, like sheep, have strayed away. We have left God's paths to follow our own. Yet the Lord laid on him the sins of us all" (NLT). What an inheritance for those who receive his gift of salvation! "Let the redeemed of the Lord say so, Whom He has redeemed from the hand of the enemy" (Ps. 107:2 NKJV).

Health Words

"The tongue of the wise promotes health."
—Proverbs 12:18 NKJV

"Pay attention, my child, to what I say. Listen carefully. Don't lose sight of words. Let them penetrate deep within your heart, for they bring life and radiant health to anyone who discovers their meaning."
—Proverbs 4:20–22 NLT

"He sent His word and healed them and delivered them from destruction."
—Psalm 107:20 NKJV

"In the beginning was the Word, and the Word was with God, and the Word was God" (John 1:1 NIV). The living Word is Jesus. He was the express image of God. Jesus told Philip, "Anyone who has seen me has seen the Father" (John 14:9 NIV).

We also have the written Word, God's book of instruction and love letter to his followers. The fifty-third chapter of the book of Isaiah reveals what Jesus' sacrifice of his body provided for anyone who would believe in him: "But he was pierced for our rebellion, crushed for our sins. He was beaten so we could be whole. He was whipped so we could be healed. All of us, like sheep, have strayed away. We have left God's

paths to follow our own. Yet the Lord laid on him the sins of us all"
(Isa. 53:5–6 NLT).

Praise Words

The Bible contains thrilling accounts of victory following praise.
The fall of Jericho recorded in Joshua chapter six is one example when
the people shouted as loud as they could when they heard the rams'
horns. After they watched the walls of Jericho collapse, the Israelites
charged in and captured it. The power of praise cannot be overstated.
It brings God on the scene.

In adverse situations I try to remember to praise with words like
these:

> "I will trust you God. I know you will bring good out of this. I know
> your power is greater than that of the Evil One. I know you will with-
> hold no good thing from those who walk uprightly. I know you cause
> me to triumph in Christ Jesus and you have given me power over the
> Enemy. I have the keys to the Kingdom, and whatever I bind on earth
> will be bound in heaven, and whatever I loose on earth will be loosed
> in heaven. What Satan means for evil you will turn to good."

Praise did not come naturally to me. Others would say, "Praise the
Lord," and I would think, "What for?" I prayed for a spirit of praise. I
had to learn to cultivate that spirit by forming a habit of remembering
what the Lord did in previous situations when I cried out to him to
help me with the things I faced. "Therefore, let us offer through Jesus
a continual sacrifice of praise to God, proclaiming our allegiance to his
name" (Heb. 13:15 NLT). Praise comes more freely when we have been
Christians for some time and seen his hand of provision over and over.

Power in the Declared Word

Daniel is a man who believes strongly in the power of words.
After living as a single man for forty years, often feeling lonely and

with no prospects of a wife, he took Word action. Daniel looked up biblical passages about marriage and the qualities of a godly wife. These passages included Proverbs 31:11–12 (NLT) "Who can find a virtuous and capable wife? She is worth more than precious rubies. Her husband can trust her, and she will greatly enrich his life."

The writer of the proverb also says, "She is clothed with strength and dignity, and she laughs without fear of the future. When she speaks, her words are wise, and she gives instructions with kindness. She carefully watches everything in her household and suffers nothing from laziness. Her children stand and bless her. Her husband praises her: 'There are many virtuous and capable women in the world, but you surpass them all!' Charm is deceptive, and beauty does not last; but a woman who fears the Lord will be greatly praised. Reward her for all she has done. Let her deeds publicly declare her praise" (31:25–31 NLT).

Daniel started declaring these words aloud with the belief: "The Lord has a wife for me and she is coming." He started making improvements in his house to make it more attractive and livable for a wife. He daily quoted aloud the scriptures pertaining to his single state, knowing that the Lord said, "It is not good for the man to be alone. I will make a helper who is just right for him" (Gen. 2:18 NLT).

After about four months he met his future wife, Jane. They were engaged within three days as the Lord confirmed to Daniel, "This is your wife." The marriage took place in six weeks. Daniel became a husband, a son-in-law, and a step-parent. Within a couple of years he became the grandparent of a lovely little girl whom he adores. It has been marvelous to see the Lord work as Jane and Daniel have trusted him.

Daniel did not sit around hoping for a wife or feeling sorry for himself. He sought the Word of the Lord and filled the atmosphere around him with God's promises. Daniel believes God's will is established on earth by the use of words—words that are in line with the divine will as revealed in the words of Scripture.

The Lord was working in Jane at the same time. She had written a description of the qualities she desired in a husband before she met Daniel. He fit them perfectly. Needless to say this is an unusual story of God directing two people to each other in such a short time and was unique for them. Daniel and Jane were very mature spiritually and were confident of God's directing them. Time has proven this as Daniel and Jane have been happily married for a number of years.

In his daily Web devotional, Tommy Hays (www.messiahministries. com, September 22, 2004) says, "Our words tend to reveal our hearts. Even those who tend to be very controlled in their speech and very careful in the image they portray, eventually their hearts are revealed in the words they speak. Of course, we all convey as much with the look of our eyes and the expression of our faces as with the words that come out of our mouths."

Suggested Prayer

Lord, purify our hearts so that you may purify our words. Let our words release life to one another and to ourselves, rather than death. Let us bless rather than curse. Let us praise rather than condemn. We are created in your image and you have entrusted incredible power to us to create or destroy through the words we speak. Amen.

Reflection

1. Are you carrying the memory of unkind words spoken over you? How can you rid yourself of them?

2. Can you recall specific words that have affirmed you? What are they?

3. How do you guard the words you speak to others?

4. Do you believe words can have a profound influence on others? Why or why not?

Chapter 7

HEALTHY FRIENDSHIPS

Many readers may have come out of troubled backgrounds with no pattern of healthy friendships. As they believe in and follow the Lord Jesus Christ, he longs to be their friend, as well as their Savior. The following ideas offer suggestions to help in forming healthy relationships with others. It is written from the viewpoint of an older Christian looking back on experiences I have walked through and lessons I am continuing to learn.

Close friendships are wonderful gifts, which help fill a need deep within us to feel connected. Each friendship takes on a personality of its own, as we come to accept that various friends fill different roles in our lives. We can't "recast" a friend to meet every need that may arise in our life situations. We learn what each friend is comfortable with and what behavior we can expect. Each individual is unique, with qualities that will enrich our lives if we can learn to accept those areas we do not find attractive. Hopefully we will also find this acceptance extended back to us.

Talents and Giftings

One great benefit found in friendship is that we can affirm each other in our talents. We make room for our friends to grow in their gifting even if it overshadows or duplicates our own gift. As Paul wrote, "Encourage each other and build each other up, just as you are already doing" (1 Thess. 5:11 NLT). It is exciting and gratifying when we have the opportunity to encourage others in "trying their wings" in a specific area where we discern they have latent abilities. Often they feel wobbly and unsure of themselves, but with encouragement and prayer I have seen several muster up the courage to step forth. Following this advance they experience the exuberance of knowing that God is using them to represent him on earth to shed his love and presence to his creation. It is wonderful to watch this happen.

For too long many of us have tried to fit ourselves or others into vacant spots of work or service that do not really suit us. On the flip side, sometimes we grow as we step out in areas we have not tried, and we are amazed to discover hidden fits. The balance between being reluctant to do something because it doesn't fit, and being reluctant to do something because of timidity, is a fine line. This may be discerned by being willing to follow that inner leading we all experience from time to time. A good friend who knows you well can act as a sounding board in confirming the action you think you are to take.

Strengths/Weaknesses

See each friend as unique and focus on all of their strengths rather than the areas perceived as weaknesses. We are all in varying stages of growth; often we are immature in areas where others have grown up and matured. It helps to remember that each of us has weaknesses. If we have made the decision to follow Christ, then these will be corrected as God teaches and trains us in these areas. Often the Lord uses challenges in friendships to do a refining work in us. "Always be humble and gentle. Be patient with each other, making allowance for each other's faults because of your love. Make every effort to keep yourselves united in the Spirit, binding yourselves together with peace" (Eph. 4:2–3 NLT). It is a blessing to have friends that know you "to the core," weaknesses and all, yet still accept and love you and call forth the best in you. True friends can be honest with each other, but not in hurtful ways. "Let your conversation be gracious and attractive so that you will have the right response for everyone" (Col. 4:6 NLT). For

Christians this honesty can be touchy when one or the other is not following scriptural principles and we are led to bring this to the attention of our friend. I am not referring to nitpicking over every area of life. I am referring to behavior where basic biblical principles are being disregarded, principles that war against various sins. Among these are: unforgiveness of others, taking offense, and bitterness. These issues also block clear friendship communication.

It is helpful to pray for our friendships, asking God to guard our hearts and the hearts of our friends against attacks from the enemy. These attacks could be in the form of jealousy or harsh words spoken in haste, which can open an opportunity for taking offense. Pray that the lines of communication remain open. And pray for new friendships. Be led by God in responding to the needs of those coming across your path. Be open to new people as sometimes God puts people together for a purpose.

Allowing ourselves to be vulnerable can draw people to us and make us more approachable. We do not have to project to others that we have it all together. Two of the most recognized women Bible teachers of today (Anne Graham Lotz and Beth Moore) are very open about their own personal struggles. Close friendships require nurturing. We learn to put ourselves in our friend's mind-set and base our actions on the things that are important to them. We need to be quick to listen to what their heart is saying and not necessarily just to what is coming out of their mouth.

We can pray to have a close friend who is further along in the Christian life than we are. We also need to be sensitive to those we may be called to mentor. This may take the form of informal sharing of spiritual truths as specific situations arise, or as a structured mentoring program. We need to be sure we keep Scripture as our basis for advice rather than reinforcing misconceptions the ones we are mentoring have picked up along life's journey.

Honesty

True friends will not reinforce each other in wrong attitudes and thinking. They will guard against taking up offenses against anyone who has mistreated their friend. Good friends, who are emotionally healthy and strive to live by scriptural principles, will encourage each other to embrace the teachings of Jesus regarding forgiveness and encourage then not to hold on to offenses. They will pray for and with us, and help us to deal with offenses so that "no one misses the grace of God and that no bitter root grows up to cause trouble and defile many" (Heb. 12:15 NIV). I have found it helpful to listen and acknowledge my friends' pain in a situation, let them vent their feelings, and then gently point to the scriptures on offense and forgiveness.

Healthy Dependence

The basis of a healthy friendship is rooted in our own relationship with God. The only constant, eternal, never-fail friend is Jesus Christ. Scripture assures us that God has said, "I will never fail you. I will never abandon you" (Heb. 13:5 NLT). According to the letter to the Colossians, the more our roots go down deep in Christ, the more we are rooted and built up in him, strengthened in the faith as we were taught, and overflowing with thankfulness (Col. 2:7). The more our Christian roots go down, the less need we will have to depend on friends to meet the deep needs which only our Creator can satisfy.

We need to seek discernment to know when our friends are relying on us to meet their own deep needs. Many of us have a tendency to want others to take care of us in the emotional realm, and also a drive to take care of others, manifesting as thinking we have to have answers for those in perplexing situations. But we must be certain to keep our friends and ourselves dependent on God first and foremost. There is a fine line between dong this and having a tender, sympathetic, and ministering heart to a friend's pain. This is best accomplished by listening patiently without judgment, and then praying with them while incorporating scriptural guidelines. Learn to use discernment in choosing those in whom you confide. The pain we are experiencing at the moment may cause us to talk indiscriminately to everyone within earshot. But it is wise to seek out a trusted friend who will pray over troubling situations and keep them confidential.

Keep pointing your friend to God so he or she does not become too dependent upon you. We can guard against an unhealthy co-dependent relationship on both sides of the friendship. We may need to check to be sure we are not encouraging dependency because it feeds something in us. One critical area in which to be alert is self-worth (labeled self-esteem by psychologists). A constant need to be built up by friends signals a problem with self-image. Our Creator is the best source for discovering who we are, both through what his Word says about his children and through prayer.

Spiritual gift assessments can be very helpful. We are best equipped to effectively serve in the Kingdom when we know and acknowledge our giftings and talents and use them. It is not boastful to say, "This is what I do best." In fact, we may have a false humility that keeps us from stepping up for service in areas where we are gifted—whether in church or community. We may think others will see us as boastful or pushy if we volunteer to serve in our areas of giftedness. Satan tries to trick us into holding back in serving where others could be blessed by the talents with which we have been entrusted.

Empathy

Be quick to listen and slow to offer advice. Remember that many people just need someone to listen. Many times the answer becomes clear as we talk about a situation. Help your friend tap resources through praying and giving any practical help you can. If you need to speak into the situation make sure that you have a sound spiritual principle for what you say. Make it clear if you are giving advice developed out of your own opinions. An empathizing presence that helps us touch God through prayer is often all that is needed to overcome troubling life situations.

Confrontation

There are times when a friend must be confronted in order to salvage the friendship. One example is that a friend may have a tendency to call too early in the morning just to talk, or perhaps too late at night, not respecting the schedule of the person they are calling. My husband is a "night owl" and may be awakened out of a sound sleep by friends who call me too early.

Rachel told me she was going through a very challenging situation with a family member when a good friend of many years came down hard on her. She wanted to break all connection with her friend and write her off. This had been a long-time pattern of Rachel's in response to people with whom she has had conflicts. She considered all of the years of their friendship and asked herself, "Do I want all of these years of close friendship with which we have been blessed to be overridden by this one isolated incident?"

Rachel called and set a time to talk with her friend, expressing how much the friendship had meant to her over the years. Then she said, "When I came to you with my pain I needed a listening ear, not a sermon." "I am so sorry," the friend answered. They talked it out and the threat to the friendship was repelled.

Rachel continues to count this woman as a dear friend. She feels so blessed that she didn't allow her hurt to cause a breach in their friendship. The friendship became stronger as it weathered this challenge.

Jealousy

Jealously of other people with whom your friend has friendships can also be a threat. One lady told me that she has to be very careful with one friend not to mention the activities that she engages in with other friends. The friend is so insecure that she becomes quite jealous. Group activities that include this particular friend pose problems and are often not attempted. There is no freedom extended to enjoy other friendships. This, of course, is very restricting. I suggest continuing to invite this friend to share in group functions while making sure someone pays her attention if she chooses to come. Otherwise we are not helping her deal with her insecurity.

Disappointment in Friendships

We can extend mercy when friends disappoint us and do not meet our expectations. Perhaps they may need to grow in the area in question or perhaps we need to be more mature in our expectations. I am learning to guard against placing specific expectations on friends. Allow others the freedom to say they cannot help in a situation without getting your feelings hurt. Accept help from people God will send along to help you. Friendships need to be fluid—give and take. Holding a friendship too tightly will stifle it.

Enduring friendships require nurturing. It helps to remember that we all have our own set of "baggage"—things that may not have been exposed, but are still beneath the surface and influencing our behavior. Extend mercy to your friends when they disappoint you and know that you will often be in need of mercy extended back to you. Many of us have experienced painful breaks with Christian friends. Sometimes we have tried everything we know to restore the former relationship, but to no avail. We remain perplexed over the reason we have been shut out from what we thought was a close friendship.

Reasons Friendships Fail or Change

In vulnerable moments sometimes friends reveal too many details of a personal nature. They then become uncomfortable with your knowledge and tend to avoid you. One counselor told me of a situation where a lady transported a friend for an abortion (although she was not in agreement with this decision). Now the person who had the abortion will not even look at her former friend when they happen to pass each other.

Another story involved a woman who revealed a lot of details involving abuse by her father as she grew up. After this disclosure the friendship that had been very close suddenly just evaporated. The friend she had confided in was perplexed and tried everything to "reconnect," but did not succeed. It was years later before she discerned that the friend was probably embarrassed that she had shared such intimate details and this was probably the cause of the broken relationship.

Perhaps you supported a friend through a very troubling, painful time. Later that friend may subconsciously associate you with that period. When she moves on into a happier time of her life you are a silent reminder of the situation she endured. As she leaves the sadness behind, she also leaves your friendship behind.

There are times a Christian friend will not accept the standard of godly principles that you hold up for her as a guide for his or her actions. In spite of trying to point out the consequences of the friend's choices, they go headlong into a sinful situation that has serious repercussions. We need to make sure we are using appropriate Scripture and speaking the truth in love as we express our concerns and cautions in a spirit of love. "Instead, speaking the truth in love, we will in all things grow up into him who is the Head, that is, Christ" (Eph. 4:15 NLT). If the friend does not listen, Scripture tells us to take another believer with us to address the situation: "If your brother sins against you, go and show him his fault, just between the two of you. If he listens to you, you have won your brother over. But if he will not listen, take one or two others along, so that 'every matter may be established by the testimony of two or three witnesses'" (Matt. 18:15–16 NIV).

Undoubtedly, the easiest reason that friendships fail or change is that God moves one or the other involved in the friendship into a different season of life or ministry. This falls under the heading of change rather than failure, but it can be painful. It is wise to accept this and remain open to the new people God brings across our paths. We should make every effort to be flexible in our relationships. We may miss many blessings if we do not keep an open attitude toward those we meet. One lady told me that upon meeting a new person she always thinks, "I wonder what God will add to me through this person?" And, of course, it is always appropriate to wonder what God will add to another person through you. Each person is uniquely made and has his or her own contributions to make in a relationship.

We may have been used by God to minister to a person and now our time of involvement is over. Perhaps we were part of God's overall plan for this person's salvation or discipleship or healing. The assignment is passed on to someone else for the next step. It is important to discern this and try not to hold on tightly to the relationship. We have to be ready to free the person to bond with the next individual God puts in their path.

Inner Circle

We can only have a very limited "inner circle" of friends. This inner circle consists of those with whom we are in an accountability relationship and to whom we give "permission" to give us advice. We remain open, however, to other friendships God may bring. But guard your heart from a steady stream of people who may bring confusion by attempting to indiscriminately speak their opinions into significant areas of your life.

This inner circle is where we are committed to "speak the truth in love" with no superiority, judgment or condemnation. We encourage each other to guard our hearts and walk in love seeing that "no one misses the grace of God and that no bitter root grows up to cause trouble and defile many" (Heb. 12:15 NIV).

God as Friend

The only constant, eternal, never-fail friend is the Lord Jesus Christ. Hebrews 13:5 says that Jesus' love for us is great, and because of that, "Never will I leave you; never will I forsake you" (NIV). It takes discipline and practice to learn to lay out our problems before God in prayer before calling a friend. In other words, we must call on the throne before we call on the phone. Then we may seek godly counsel/suggestions from others to test what we are feeling and hearing. This can be a difficult habit to establish, as it is human nature to seek sympathy and to want to portray ourselves to others as the "injured" party. We need to check our advice by scriptural principles so friends do not become too dependent upon us. We have to be sure any dependency is not feeding some need we have.

Close friendships are wonderful gifts from God, and as such they require nurturing. I am trying to learn to put myself in my friend's shoes and lay my own preferences aside if need be. We all have our growing edges. The challenges in friendships can do a refining work within us as we learn to extend forgiveness in the times others disappoint us. But close enduring friendships are a cause for celebration!

Dealing with Feelings

Many of us deny and push away the emotions we experience over fractured friendships. We may think a mature person would not let this kind of thing bother them, so we refuse to admit there is a problem. Thus the accompanying pain is pushed away or gets buried. Another way some of us deal with the feelings of challenges in our friendships is to spew negative remarks over anyone near us, thus degrading and slandering the other person involved.

We are responsible for doing everything we can to walk in clear relationships with friends. If they will not respond when we ask for forgiveness, then we have done our part and the responsibility goes over to them.

Acknowledge the pain involved. Bring it to light by talking to the heavenly Father. For those of us who are Christians we can cry out our hurt in prayer and tell God everything we are feeling and thinking and soak in his healing light. Lay all the hurt before God, tell him every detail and every disappointment you are experiencing related to the situation. It is much better to have a "pity party" with God in prayer than to indulge in one alone or with a friend. We need to release the pain and hurt and stop it from festering. If it is a deep hurt we may have to pray over it a number of times before it can be completely released.

Often the hurtful things that are underneath in all of us never get dealt with—they just get cut off and then they grow back. In real life, roots left in the soil continue to grow, and so it is with things in our spirits. If they are only cut off, the roots are still hidden in the dirt and will grow back. If the roots are pulled out and held up to the light of Jesus Christ, they will die for lack of nourishment provided by "dirt."

It is important to ask for forgiveness if we know we have wronged another. Ask, "Will you forgive me?" If they will not, then we are free from further responsibility. There are times when nothing will restore the relationship. Then we have to move on, being sure not to harbor ill will toward the person. The writer of the New Testament book of Hebrews told us to "Make every effort to live in peace with all men and to be holy; without holiness no one will see the Lord. See to it that no one misses the grace of God and that no bitter root grows up to cause trouble and defile many" (Heb. 12:14–15 NIV). We receive a great blessing by choosing to lay down hurt and walk peacefully in the freedom made possible by Jesus, the Prince of Peace.

Many of these suggestions for dealing with feelings are appropriate for a work environment. Remember that everyone is to some extent part of the "walking wounded." We can pray that God will let us see people through his eyes, but it is not our job to right all of the wrongs we see in others or in the environment. That would be futile and would just wear anyone out. Besides, God can do a better job.

Bob was a man who did not use care in selecting his friends, and it was disastrous. He recounts, "I wanted approval and acceptance, and my rebellion got out of hand! I guess we think going with the flow is the easiest way to gain approval and acceptance. Unfortunately, I became a hellion and went through a time in my life when sin meant nothing to me and I would try just about anything.

"There are a lot of things I won't ever do again. I pretty much tried it all. I did drugs, alcohol, you name it. I had stringy long hair and an unkept scraggy looking beard. After four knee operations, I thought I was tough. Actually, I was cruel and callous. I was a wretch. I played the role, but then the role started playing me.

"The real me was seeking approval any way I could. Most of my time was spent trying to be cool for girls. You had to have money to impress them, so my friends and I bought a bunch of candy canes and went door to door offering them in exchange for a donation for the nativity scene down at the local church. People responded so well we bought the store out of candy canes. How gullible those people were. Forget the nativity scene! We bought beer and chased girls with the money. We were even brazen enough to go to the Catholic Newman Center and 'borrow' vestments for nuns and priests. My friend and I posed as Sister Tonette and Father Ron and went through the girl's dorm offering our services as members of the clergy. We were even sacrilegious enough to do mock baptisms in the river to amuse them.

"I waited tables at a local saloon and learned to tend bar, hire bands, and throw drunken parties. My involvement with foul language, smoking, drinking, and drugs developed even further when some of us went into partnership and bought a nightclub—one complete with topless dancers from five to nine and rock-n-roll bands from nine to closing. What a nightmare: drunk employees, half-naked women, musicians on drugs, and deafeningly loud music. I developed a terrible alcohol problem, and sometimes I would have twenty or more bourbon-and-waters a night. At the end of the night I would do more drugs to stay awake to drive home. I did uppers, downers, and pot. I thought I was a real leader, but looking back I was a cowardly follower.

"The nightclub broke my parents' heart. They were kind, gentle Christian people, always ready to serve their Lord and neighbors. They called me to their home to confront me. My mother had the newspaper ad for the club lying on her lap on top of her Bible. She lamented that I was keeping men from being at home with their families. I said, 'Mom, it is just business.'

"One night this cute brunette came to the night club. I fell for her and in six months we were married. When people questioned how I got such a prize, I just said, 'I lie and keep her drunk.' Then the crisis came. My brother's house burned to the ground. He and his family escaped by crawling out on their hands and knees. I was devastated and went the next morning to sift through the cold and frozen rubble. I saw a reflection from the sun and I dusted off a mirror on which these words were inscribed: 'Let your life so shine before men that you may be a reflection of God.' I pulled through the heap where the roof and ceiling had burned and collapsed in the living room and discovered a marble table covered with ashes. On that table was an open Bible that had not even been scorched!

"Through the tears I looked up at a perfectly blue sky and said, 'I give up. Whatever it is you want from me, God, I am yours.' There I was, freezing, alone, on top of ashes, and God showed up. His presence was so real. After I got ambushed by God I started asking things like, 'Who and what will be the center of my life?' 'Who will I live for?' 'What will I build my life around?'

"The leader of a church men's group I joined showed me that commitment is vital. He told me to make my commitment to God so strong that it will hold me together when life starts breaking apart. The group has provided the healthy friendships I needed. Then he talked about my commitment to my wife. Her beauty, wisdom, and compassion keep me motivated. I have a mental video that I play to keep me serving and honoring her so that I do not do something stupid. That video is her boarding a plane holding hands and laughing with another man. That just can't happen. Try it men; it will help keep you faithful.

"My toughest challenge was looking at myself in the mirror. I realized how ugly my behavior had been. I started to emulate the good traits in leaders around me. I found they didn't talk about others, use fiery words, cuss, drink, smoke, or cheat on their wives. They just lived life real and clean.

"I thought of myself as the son in the biblical parable in Luke chapter fifteen who took his inheritance and left home for riotous living. He ended up busted and empty. That was me. I was the Prodigal Son now come home to his father. I was baptized and, of all things, the man who posed as Sister Tonette was baptized the same day. Many readers will know the feeling of coming up through that clear water of the baptistery, representing a fresh start and a new life. I never want to go back!

"What are some lessons I learned from being such an idiot? I learned you can shed bad habits. One night I was running around in the bedroom and stumped my toe on the door jam. The pain raced through my body. I was overjoyed that I did not cuss, and fell on the bed laughing at the freedom. And I learned that in human logic you can't get from here to there. You just can't. But because of Christ, you can. My biggest problem is that I have to take 'me' everywhere I go! I have to ask God what I need to surrender and what in my life is keeping me stuck.

"I learned that the goal in sex is not conquering, to feel good, and to brag to friends. Those hot hormones lead to things you think you have to do and that the minute it is over you feel bad and uncomfortable, and as you walk away you feel yucky, lonely, and depressed. I also learned about respect and faithfulness, and I want to pass that on to my daughters. I challenged them to stay pure, to save themselves for marriage. I coach them in the ways guys will try to lure them. They each have a ring as a reminder of what they are trying to do. They were both inspired by a Miss America, who said to competitors who made fun of her for being a virgin, 'In sixty seconds I can be like you, but you can never be like me.'

"Thanks to a God of second chances, a God who built a new fire in me. I keep working on me to serve him better because I'm not yet the man I want to be. But thank God I'm not the man I used to be. I thank the Lord for the godly men he has connected me with who serve as role models and keep me accountable to live a pure life."

Suggested Prayer

God, please help me not to seek out friends just to entertain myself or fill a void within that should be reserved for you. Lead me to the friends with whom you want me to connect. Give me the wisdom to treasure each friend as your unique creation. Help me to be sensitive and to guard my friendships. In the name of Jesus I pray. Amen.

Reflection

1. Do you have friends who try to draw out of you in unhealthy ways? What ways?

2. If you are burdened by the demands of some of your friends, how are you burdened?

3. How do you try to see each friend as unique?

4. Are you selective with who you share your confidences? How did you learn to be this way?

Chapter 8

SURRENDER THE BURDEN

The words of Jesus' invitation still ring out today: "Come to me, all of you who are weary and carry heavy burdens, and I will give you rest. Take my yoke upon you. Let me teach you, because I am humble and gentle at heart, and you will find rest for your souls. For my yoke is easy to bear, and the burden I give you is light" (Matt. 11:28–30 NLT).

The Root of the Problem

One of the greatest challenges we face in life is surrendering our self-will. I am not speaking of the initial surrender we make when committing our lives to Jesus. Rather, I am speaking of the defiant "self" that continues springing up in various situations. The very heart of the issue of surrendering lies in subduing the self-protective, self-assertive, and totally self-centered nature with which we were born. As we mature and our horizon expands, we are challenged to move beyond this infant state.

Areas of Surrender

TIME

We must surrender our time. As followers of Christ we have to resolve to stop and be used to advance the Kingdom wherever God provides an opportunity. It is a discipline not to be so focused on our own agenda and plans that we walk past those who are suffering, or who need a kind word or helping hand. In our hustle-bustle society it is very touching to witness random acts of kindness. It also is a way to transmit the love of Jesus to a hurting world. The Christian represents Christ's presence on the earth as his Spirit is given full range to move through those who desire to be used in this manner and who will make themselves available.

MONEY/MATERIAL THINGS

Material things must be surrendered. They can occupy too great a place in our lives if we are not careful to keep our priorities straight. Giving ten percent of their increase was what the people of God practiced in the Old Testament. The term for this is *tithing*. Malachi 3:10–11 says to "'Bring all the tithes into the storehouse so there will be enough food in my Temple. If you do,' says the Lord of Heaven's Armies, 'I will open the windows of heaven for you. I will pour out a blessing so great you won't have enough room to take it in! Try it! Put me to the test! Your crops will be abundant, for I will guard them from insects and disease. Your grapes will not fall from the vine before they are ripe,' says the Lord of Heaven's Armies" (NLT). Tithing opens the windows of heaven for the pouring out of great blessings.

Our motive for giving should not be in order to receive back. Still, in Luke 6:38 Jesus says to "Give, and you will receive. Your gift will return to you in full—pressed down, shaken together to make room for more, running over, and poured into your lap. The amount you give will determine the amount you get back" (NLT). Abundance will return to those who give generously. But one's giving extends far beyond money as it may involve acts of kindness and various types of help given at just the right time.

IMAGE

"Our self image and the way we appear to others are perhaps the most difficult of all things for us to surrender. Even when we give our lives and everything else to Christ, we feel we must look good both to ourselves and to our community of friends."[1]

While we all want to be looked on with favor by others, it is helpful to make up our minds that God is the one we need to please by living by his standards as set forth in Scripture. Others may misunderstand us, but we can examine our motives and keep a clear conscience.

CHILDREN

It came to me one day when my children were growing up and I was dogmatically laying down the law to one of them: "You are doing this because of the way it will make you look to the neighbors if Johnny doesn't toe the line." It was a flash of insight. What a jolt, but it was true.

The issue of children offers a real challenge to many of us. We want to be good parents, and we try hard to do the things and provide the experiences we think will enrich their lives. We want them to love and serve the Lord. Then one day the little sheep start leaving the safety of the home pasture. They may become infatuated and indoctrinated with ideas and customs foreign to their parents. They may walk away from the teaching we tried so hard to instill in them. It is especially troubling to have them turn from their spiritual roots.

Whether babies, toddlers, school age, or adults, our children can actually become idols to us if we are not careful. Our desire to turn out a "good product" can affect the way we raise a child. For grown children, we may attempt to control them in a way that masquerades as "I just want the best for them." We fail to remember that what is best in the short term is not always the best in the long term.

EXPECTATIONS

In addition to surrendering control over our adult children, we become freer as we surrender the expectations others have of us and are not obsessed with trying to mold ourselves into these expectations. We all have our own unique personality and way of responding in different situations. We should not expect others to view things exactly the way we do. No one thinks and reacts exactly the same way as others. We save ourselves a lot of grief when we respect the individuality of each person and do not try to force anyone to behave in ways we think appropriate. Of course we expect to extend and receive common courtesy.

It helps to learn that our way is not the only way. In fact, not only is our way not the only way, it may not necessarily be the best way to do things. Others may actually have a better idea on an issue, so we must respect other opinions and give people the courtesy of being heard.

RELATIONSHIPS

Surrendering relationships is sometimes very difficult, and the tighter we hold on to other people the more they struggle to free themselves.

Ann shared some profound thoughts on surrender as she struggled to find peace over a broken relationship. The young man who had declared his undying love and desire to marry her backed away. She was mystified and deeply grieved. One of the scriptures that ministered to her at that time was, "You open your hand and satisfy the desires of every living thing" (Ps. 145:16 NIV). "A key element of surrendering to God involved recognizing my own desires. Before I could 'let go' of any dream, grudge, or want that I had, I literally laid out all of my desires before God—on paper. I named every desire I had and how I wanted my life to be psychologically, physically, emotionally, and spiritually in order to help identify what needed to change and be healed.

"Once I clearly identified these desires, I stepped back and realized that what I feared was that what God had planned for my life would fall short of all I had desired. Somehow I was afraid my desires were too great for God. Through prayer I came to understand that the exact opposite was true, that no matter how big and great my desires are, what God has planned is much bigger and much greater. If he were to fulfill all of my desires for a husband exactly as I envisioned, they would still be only a burning match compared to a blazing bonfire of intimacy that is possible with God. In a deeper understanding and true acceptance of God's plan for me lies the power to really surrender."

"He is the 'I am' that implies present fellowship and safety. … If you are distressed over anything it means that you are not fully surrendered to God's will, although it may seem to you that you are living according to His will. She who lives according to God's will has no cares. If she is in need of something, she offers herself and the thing she wants to God, and if she does not receive it she remains as tranquil as if she had gotten what she wanted."[2]

Following the complete relinquishment of Ann's relationship as she embraced God's will, the Lord did eventually send her a wonderful husband. I have experienced over and over the power in letting go. I believe God starts working when we yield a situation to him and let him take over. In issues of control God does not like our hands gripping people or situations.

Healing of Resentments

Joan's story illustrates the power of the truth expressed in Psalm 55:22: "Give your burdens to the Lord, and he will take care of you. He will not permit the godly to slip and fall" (NLT). "Throughout my life I have experienced deep hurt and resentment toward members of my own family. From early childhood I was amazed that people who were supposed to love you the most were often self-absorbed, callous, and sometimes cruel. Anger festered in me like a cancer. I prayed to God to release me from the pain and let me forgive. I could not find that release because deep down I felt justified in my anger. I had a right to be angry! I grew weary of being misunderstood and treated unfairly.

"Relinquishment came to me when I could honestly say before God, 'My way leads to destruction. I want your will to be done in my life, Lord, no matter what happens to me. I want you to be able to say to me some day, "Well done, thou good and faithful servant."' As I have walked with my heart and mind on honoring my heavenly Father by my words and actions, I have begun to see some of my family situations change. God has poured his love through me to touch my sister's life. A few years ago I did not know if I could ever love her again. I stand in awe of what God can do if I am willing to let go. He has given me peace and mercy toward my sister. These are both from the Father, lest I dare boast.

"I love the old hymns. In my meditation I sing those ageless words, 'I'd rather have Jesus than anything this word affords today—the things of this earth will grow strangely dim, in the light of His glory and grace.' His Word holds me fast. When I slip, I can be regrounded by His promise, 'I will never leave you or forsake you.' Praise him! His love endures forever."

Carol Kent writes that, "We can hug our hurts and make a shrine out of our sorrows, or we can offer them to God as a sacrifice of praise. The choice is ours."[3] She continues: "But when we release our grasp, our relinquishment puts a stop to the manipulation of other people and releases the Holy Spirit to do the supernatural through the power of prayer. It is an act of trusting God when we cannot envision a positive outcome."[4]

Surrendering Habits and Addictions

Linda was bound to a twenty-year habit of smoking two packs of cigarettes a day. She knew the health dangers and longed to stop. Her husband was also a heavy smoker. After he developed bladder cancer, his life depended on him giving up cigarettes. Linda was torn between quitting to support her husband and still wanting to smoke because the cigarettes were like an old friend. When Linda was stressed she could lean on them and she really enjoyed smoking. Yet, she wanted badly to quit so she could be free. She also knew that smoking was not God's best for her. But she was afraid of failure. Paul described her when he said in Romans 7:21, "So I find this law at work: When I want to do good, evil is right there with me" (NIV).

Linda made up her mind to stop smoking. That is just what she did with the help of God, whom she had invited into her life many years previously. She just stopped! No relapses! Linda said she took all pressure off herself for a week, knitting and doing things she liked to do, as well as spending extra time in prayer. She created a nurturing environment where the stresses of life could not lure her to reach for a cigarette and light it without thinking. Her family was very understanding and supported her during this time. She had a relaxed atmosphere where she could rest, pray, and do things she liked to do. If she did not want to do the laundry, she let it go. Through the grace of God she made it through the week and has never picked up another cigarette. Now when she sees someone with a cigarette she praises the Lord for the way he set her free.

Sam's addiction had adverse effects on all of his family. He had a wonderful childhood with great parents and grandparents. He grew up in a middle-class Kentucky family. He writes, "I became a Christian when I was twelve years old. I attended college and early on knew I wanted to be a teacher and a coach. These dreams were fulfilled as I taught math, was an assistant basketball coach, and head golf coach. I married and had two wonderful children. Life was good and I rose to a place of prominence in the small town, serving as an elder in the church, as a city council and school board member, and was active in other endeavors in the community.

"But there was a common thread in my life that had started at about the age of six and intensified as I got older—gambling. I made bets on the golf course, shooting pool, and playing poker, and I continued this into my college years and my professional career. I was good in sports and I loved to watch them, and now I could get some easy money by betting on ball games. I thought it was okay because society said it was. There was the lottery, horse racing, poker, Las Vegas, and so on, so why not bet on sports as long as I didn't bet too much?

"Then things changed when I lost money I didn't have. I had to borrow two thousand dollars to pay off a debt and I didn't tell my wife.

Deceit, cover up, and lying started. I had to win to pay this loan. I hated that I had to use work money to pay it back.

"This trend continued for years, and the betting increased to hundreds of dollars every day. I went to work at a bank and still continued gambling and going to 'stag' night at the country club, playing high stakes poker, and shooting dice—all for a lot of money.

"My bank partners asked me to stop the open gambling at the club, so I bet more on the ball games with a bookmaker. I couldn't stop. I loved the high it gave me. It got so bad that eventually I didn't care if I won or lost. I had to make the bet. It was like a fix.

"The bookmaker, casino, lottery, and horseracing are all like the undertaker in that they will get you in the end. The day came when I lost seven thousand dollars in one week. I used all of our home equity by lying to my wife to take a second mortgage on our home. I had stolen from our kid's savings accounts. I had no other recourse, so I made a fake loan to pay off the seven thousand dollar debt.

"I really sweated out the week, but I won enough the next week to pay it back. I kept telling myself to quit gambling. But I had a second loan to pay back, and I wasn't going to do it with our working money. I had to bet, so the illegal loans increased, the lying increased, the cover-ups increased, and I was living in a hell on earth. My head hurt and I was depressed. I didn't want to get out of bed in the morning, my stomach churned, and I couldn't concentrate. I was handcuffed in a prison and didn't know how to get out. I was slowly wasting away hiding this secret sin.

"The day finally came when I couldn't live with this any longer. I wrote a note to my wife listing all of the loans at the bank. I told her how much I loved her and the kids but that I had shamed them and my community and my God and I had to go—they would be better off without me. I left with a gun and drove around for eight hours battling the loud voice raging in my head, 'Do it, do it, do it.' Yet a small voice kept saying, 'Trust me.'

"My wife found the note and called the police and my partners. I had not been able to pull the trigger, so I returned home. I went into a mental institution for three weeks, then started the twelve step recovery program. I went to prison for two years for embezzlement.

"As a convicted felon, I suffered loss of reputation, shame, loss of job and income, and loss of friends. There was money to pay back and very limited choices for the future as far as work goes. I almost lost my life, not to mention the misery I lived in every day, as well as the emotional, physical, mental, and spiritual misery and suffering because of the gambling addiction. My wife stayed with me, so the only thing I didn't lose was my family.

"Now, it feels so good to have that monster of gambling off of my back and out of my head."

To break free of habits and addictions, Sam suggests:

Begin today. Not tomorrow, not next week, today.

Accept responsibility and refuse to blame others.

Examine your life. Take an inventory of your weakness. For example, I was prideful and selfish.

Ask God to take over every area of your life—your choices, your thoughts, your billfold, your relationships, all areas.

Keep away from the temptation. Actually FLEE it.

Focus on God things so there is no vacuum in your brain. I had thoughts of gamble, gamble, gamble, until I realized something else needed to occupy my thoughts. Now I focus on God.

Restore broken relationships. Make amends to those you hurt unless it might endanger your life.

Join an accountability group.

When you have spent enough time in recovery, then give help to others who are in a similar struggle.

Dennis suffered with a different type of addiction: His life as a teenager seemed harmless to him in the 1960s when he was playing poker games with his high school friends. But alcohol and marijuana were part of those games. Stealing provided funds to continue gambling and supporting his habit of alcohol and drugs. When Dennis became a member of a music team in the US Air Force in 1970, LSD and other drugs became a part of his recreation. When he was discovered, he was considered unacceptable for any further military service and was permanently discharged from USAF within six months.

In the mid-1990s Dennis became an alcoholic while he was a university professor. His students reported to administrators that he smelled like liquor. He had believed he could drink vodka in the early morning without it being smelled by others. Not so! Dennis described his drinking as a way to mentally disappear—to get "out of his mind."

He was raised in the 1950s by parents who worshipped God. As a radical rebel, Dennis rejected any belief in God, and in the 1960s became an atheist (a belief that lasted for many decades). While a professor he dated a student who was a witch, and he became a practicing pagan. He embraced the belief that there is one god with many different religious paths to this god.

Dennis was married and divorced three times between 1970 and 1996, then in 1999 the love of his life appeared and he fell in love with her. She was strong in her Christian faith. They married despite the fact that she knew of his new age beliefs and his struggle with alcoholism. He told her that every day he was asking God to help him resolve the many violent conflicts with people that he had.

When they saw an ad for a marriage workshop at a church, they attended. The Christian leader listened to Dennis as he described the many different paths to God. The leader never seemed shocked by Dennis' beliefs and never argued with or judged him. Instead, he adopted Dennis as a close friend! This man's unconditional love was part of the miracle that contributed to Dennis' openness to the following experience:

After dark one night Dennis was walking home and the Holy Spirit of God talked to him. God's Spirit revealed to him that Jesus Christ reconciled all humans across all cultures to God through his acceptance of all their sins surrendered to him in his sacrifice to God on the cross. All people are reconciled to God if they accept Jesus Christ as their Savior, surrender their sins to him, and live their lives within his life. He was inspired with the thought that God's Holy Spirit would live within him as his guide, counselor, and path-maker to God for every moment of the rest of his life. In a mysterious way Dennis communicated with and literally experienced the true God, and he cried in joy the rest of the way home. At the age of fifty-two, his lifelong exhaustive search for truth was over. Dennis told his wife he accepted Jesus Christ and wanted to be baptized in the name of God the Father, Jesus Christ, and the Holy Spirit!

After accepting Christ and being baptized, Dennis continued drinking as a solitary drinker. He would not drink if he were away from home with other people, but when he returned home he would drink because he believed he had control over the amount he consumed. He believed every human since the sin of Adam and Eve is born with a disease leading to death, and that every Christian will be bodily resurrected in God's original perfect creation, with eternal life and no disease, when Jesus returns to earth. Dennis accepted the human definition of alcoholism as disease. It was his disease until he died, and when he died he would be bodily resurrected as God's perfect creation when Jesus returns to earth. Believing this, he continued drinking huge amounts of alcohol in his "disease" as an alcoholic.

Dennis woke up to the truth of the situation one day when he heard the Holy Spirit tell him to "Stop defining your alcoholism as a disease! Accept that it is a sin that separates your living life from God. Jesus reconciled all humans to God by bearing their sins on the cross and he invites you to surrender your sin, to give your sin to him and he will be in absolute control of your sin when you surrender it to him. Give your alcoholism to Christ as your sin; and when you surrender your alcoholism to him you will not be separated from God. Instead, you will literally experience Jesus and me living within you, and you will live your daily life in the living life of Jesus Christ."

The key to overcoming alcoholism, then, is to define and face it as a sin, not as a so-called disease. Dennis accepts this now. He came to experience that his drinking alcohol as an alcoholic was separating his heart, mind, soul, and body from God's will for him, separating him from living his life in the living life of Christ, and separating him from the guidance and counseling of the Holy Spirit.

This experience with the Holy Spirit was so profound that Dennis realized he did not want to be separated from Jesus Christ and the Holy Spirit of God who live within him and who invite him to live in the living life of Christ. His life of sin died on the cross of Christ when he surrendered it to him, was buried with him, and was resurrected with him to live a new life. Dennis experiences himself not as "recovered," but as a life reborn, reformed, and renewed in Christ.

He is still tempted to drink alcohol, but Dennis can now refuse the temptation by living his life in the living power of Jesus Christ. He says that alcohol has no place in his reborn, reformed, and renewed life. He is free from his sin of alcohol addiction. He has truth, power, and new life by surrendering the sin of alcoholism to Jesus Christ. To Satan he says, "Through my reborn, reformed, renewed life in the living life of Christ, I confidently say, 'Jesus and I do not want your temptation to me to drink alcohol again, so get away from me in his name and power. Whom Jesus Christ sets free is free indeed.'"

Remembering

A very useful tool for encouraging ourselves to lay down our burdens is found in recalling God's faithfulness to us over the years. We quiet ourselves and pull those instances up on the screens of our minds. Doing so is a great faith-builder. We remind ourselves that, "'My thoughts are nothing like your thoughts,' says the Lord. 'And my ways are far beyond anything you could imagine'" (Isa. 55:8 NLT).

For those going through troubling times, remember also Paul's often-quoted words of Romans 8:28: "And we know that God causes everything to work together for the good of those who love God and are called according to his purpose for them" (NLT). Our view is short-sighted, but God sees from the beginning to the end of our lives. We cannot know the final outcome of situations, but we can trust the Almighty God and release them into his hands.

Faithfulness of God

Linda Carruth Davis, a fellow author and friend, shared the following story: "Holy Island is the site of a serene little sea-bound village just off the northern coast of England. You must wait for the tide to go out before you can make the drive from Berwick-upon-Tweed to the shores of this place, which is also known as Lindisfarne. My sister and I made a retreat there in the spring of 1999. Walking along the rocky coastline beneath the Lindisfarne Castle, we came upon a small boat in dry dock. Its name was *Faithful*. The faithfulness of God had been powerfully illustrated to us just the day before.

"As our wee taxi cab had moved out into the ebbing tide (much too soon for my comfort) we could barely make out the little white lines dividing the two lanes of the ancient highway. Holding fast to the car door and my Bible, I was reminded of that wonderful passage from the forty-third chapter of Isaiah: 'When you pass through the waters, I will be with you' (43:2 NIV). We actually lived, in that moment, that sacred divine present moment. We were literally living in that Word and the Word was a living thing as real as the sea water on the coastland ahead. The photograph I took of that little schooner so aptly name *Faithful* sits on my desk today and reminds me of the faithfulness of the Lord in all circumstances. But there is more.

"While scavenging the beach, my sister Carol and I discovered not the usual shells one finds on a sandy shore but instead beautiful bits of china. I was reminded of my newfound interest in mosaic art and spent several happy hours collecting odd bits and pieces. The spiritual analogy fairly screams at one's mind: these broken, scattered pieces would take on new value when they become a part of a larger scheme. Their fractured value, just then in a rough and dirty state, was solely in my eyes, the artistic creator. This worth could not be known by the object nor by anyone else until the full scheme was unfolded—when the mosaic piece was completed. No stone was too small. Even the daintiest shards of china seemed to call out to me: 'Use me. Just as I am. I will have a unique place in your creation. My brokenness actually widens the scope of my usefulness as when I was a plate or a cup. That's all I was. But now I can be used, at your creative discretion, made into something new and perhaps be even better than what I was originally made to be.'

"Meditating on my own state of brokenness, I remember that day and the message of those humble bits of shattered glass."

Other Helps in Releasing Burdens

In addition to recounting the faithfulness of God in times past, I have found it helpful to take a hard look at the situation I face and ask, "Is this really my problem? Am I just trying to fix something for my own comfort, or the comfort of another?" Often I have discovered that many problems are not really mine to "fix."

In her book *Confident Woman*, Anabel Gillham describes a wonderful technique for releasing heavy burdens. She suggests getting a helium balloon, writing the burden on the balloon, and then wrapping the string from the balloon around a brick. Hold the brick out in front of you until your arm can no longer sustain the weight of it. As the brick drops, the string is released and the balloon soars and eventually disappears. One lady I know tried this. She was very grievously concerned over a relative. As her arm gave way to the weight of the brick, her burden soared into the clouds. She recounted that she heard in her spirit, "You have not released June to Satan, you have released her to me." Needless to say this situation had been prayed over thoroughly, or it would have only been a surface release and would not have stood the test of time.

The apostle Paul taught us, "Don't worry about anything; instead, pray about everything. Tell God what you need, and thank him for all he has done. Then you will experience God's peace, which exceeds anything we can understand. His peace will guard your hearts and minds as you live in Christ Jesus" (Phil. 4:6–7 NLT). Which of us would not want to experience that peace? We live in a troubled, violent, strife-filled world. To walk in peace is a great prize to be eagerly sought. With peace comes a deep restful knowing that all is well.

The prerequisite for this peace is to be found as we bring all of our needs, unrest, concerns, and anxieties to God in prayer. This is a vital step. Author and speaker Calvin Miller shares, "All in all, I'm convinced I can never take hold of anything that matters till I have let go of everything that doesn't."[5]

Suggested Prayer

God, help me to be willing to allow you to expose the areas where self is on the throne in my life. Show me where I have taken responsibility for things that are not really mine to deal with. Give me the grace to release those things to your care and leave them. Amen.

Reflection

1. What are you holding on to that may be holding you back?

2. Have you ever experienced the joy of releasing a troubling situation? What happened?

3. Which of the areas written about bother you?

4. Do you try solving problems that are not really yours? How do you do this?

Chapter 9

NO SHAME, NO CHAINS— FREE TO KNOW GOD

F ree! True freedom! It comes as we let the chains fall off as we embrace "God principles" for living. Who better to know how men and women work best than the one who created them? As mind-stretching as it seems, God knows everything about us.

Imperfect Father

Many of us grew up under various kinds of oppression. Some have lived with a single mother who had to work long hours to make ends meet. Exhausted when she came home, she was unable to fully meet the needs of her children. In other homes it is the father who has been left alone with the children, so once again the children do not receive the attention they need. Perhaps the home had two parents who were in constant conflict. Drinking, cursing, and all kinds of immoral behavior may have reared their ugly heads, stealing from the children what should have been a carefree, happy childhood.

Others of us have not only suffered neglect, but have had acts of atrocity inflicted upon us. Physical, verbal, and sexual abuse are common in many homes today. Karen relates:

"During most of my childhood I grew up in a violent home. My father abused us, as well as alcohol and drugs. On Sunday he could be found teaching Sunday school classses. I heard at church that Jesus wanted to be my Savior. I knew I needed a Savior. At home when my sibling and I would hide for safety, we would pray to Jesus to help us. Most often the hiding places worked. We were kept safe. At the age of seven I made the decision to get baptized to show that I had accepted Jesus as my Savior. Now I was a Christian!

"At this time, we left my father and lived elsewhere for safety. It was a relief to be in a less stressful environment. In the few times we did see him he was emotionally and physically abusive. It was over the course of many years that I came to know God as my real Father. I had to really let go of what an earthly father meant, based on my experiences with my own father. His mantra was, 'Be quiet, please me, and be good to make me look good.' I had to learn to rest in the true Father who tells me in his Word that I am fearfully and wonderfully made (Ps. 139:14).

"Fast-forward to having my own husband of over a decade and a half leave me to live with another woman. He seemed to be just another man that I could not please. I am now a single mom.

"I have come to understand that God created me for his pleasure. I rejoice in the fact that my heavenly Father delights in me. I live to serve him. He says, 'Follow my lead and I will show you true joy.' I have found the perfect Father, and I rest in the assurance that he is taking care of me."

Diana certainly experienced an imperfect father. He was an alcoholic who was totally self-absorbed and immature. When she was two years old, her father left home to join the navy. At that time he promised the family he would send for them as soon as he knew where he would be stationed. Years passed, and Diana overheard many conversations concerning when the family would be reunited. No definite plans were ever made. She did not see her father again until she was nine years old. After that visit he reappeared for brief periods at approximately two-year intervals. During each visit he professed love for her and the family. He held out promises of love and care, but he never followed through. She recounted how wonderful it had been to sit on his lap while being told she was "my darling little girl," and that soon he would make a home for them.

When Diana was twenty her father died while he was alone in a hotel room in Chicago. He was traveling back from South America where he had been working for a construction company. The personnel at the hotel thought he was drunk and left him alone. In reality he was suffering from a recurrence of malaria and pneumonia. Although he had been totally absent from her family's life for the previous four years, Diana's mother received the phone call from the authorities with the news of his death. Her name and contact information were found among his papers. She made the arrangements for his burial and brought his body home to West Virginia.

After being told of her father's death, Diana walked out into her neighborhood so that her mother would not see her reaction. As she paced the streets she sobbed and cried out in frustration that she would never have a father and never know a father's love. The most hurtful thing of all was the realization that he had never cared enough to get to know her. She felt she had been discounted and then discarded. It was at that time that Diana made the decision to close off any feelings or thoughts of him. She attended the funeral the next day, but she felt nothing. In fact, she decided to go to work immediately following the service, much to the dismay of her co-workers. Her kind uncle came to the workplace and told her to come with him because she should be with the rest of the family.

Over the years Diana could not break through the distance she felt in her relationship with God (although she had received Christ as her Lord and Savior). Forty years after her father's funeral, Diana was watching an old movie called *A Tree Grows in Brooklyn*. It is a film about a family with an alcoholic father who was never overtly abusive, just weak and unable to follow through with his promises. She fell to her knees, overcome by seeing her father through eyes of compassion. She understood he could not do any better. Through sobs she forgave him.

Although she was a professed believer of many years, Diana had waited a long time to embrace God as her perfect Father. She is learning that she can trust her heavenly Father, and that he will never leave her. His love is always stable and constant.

It is also significant that Diana developed a coping mechanism of holding people at arm's length. She works hard to overcome this and to not let it affect her relationship with her son and his new family. God is teaching her that she is a valuable, gifted, and unique woman.

God's Provision for Sins

When Jesus hung naked on the cross, stripped of all dignity, he took upon himself every sin, past, present, and those not yet committed. He took the penalty for the sins of all humanity upon his pierced, bleeding body. He made provision for any man, woman, or child to come into the family of God through the sacrifice of his perfect blood. "For without the shedding of blood, there is no forgiveness" (Heb. 9:22 NLT). It is an individual choice whether one will receive or refuse this gracious, unparalleled gift. Even if a person does not knowingly refuse this gift, they still have rejected it because they have not made the decision to accept Jesus' gift of eternal life. If one delays making a decision, a decision has been made by default.

Perfect Father/Parent

God is the perfect parent! He has all of the attributes of male and female with which Adam and Eve were endowed. He said he created man in his image; however, Adam and Eve had a free will which they exercised when they fell into sin by disobeying God's instructions.

As we enter into God's family we receive God as our Father. Jesus, who is our Savior, also becomes our elder brother. A vast supply of provision opens up to those who receive Jesus Christ as their personal Savior. If we make the decision to become a member of that new family we are given the power to be healed from the wounds of the past.

God, in the person of the Holy Spirit, comes to live inside those who decide to open their hearts to Christ. His spirit is the power source that enables us to forgive our imperfect parents as well as others who have inflicted great pain on us. We learn to extend forgiveness, mercy, and compassion as we let more of the Lord's character flow through us.

It is difficult for those of us who have been deeply wounded by our earthly fathers to have a true concept of God, the heavenly Father. We tend to view him the same way we view our earthly parent. Perhaps our parent punished us for the slightest infraction or provocation, which often produces a deep fear of God as a hard taskmaster. It is a big, difficult task to forgive those who, knowingly or unknowingly, left us with emotional and physical scars. Be assured that wounds inflicted by the failure of parental love can be healed! That healing is to be found in submission to Jesus and his teachings. "But for you who fear my name, the Sun of Righteousness will rise with healing in his wings. And you will go free, leaping with joy like calves let out to pasture" (Mal. 4:2 NLT). The study note of the *New Spirit-Filled Bible* states, "The Messiah is compared to a rising sun, which has visible, radiant beams of sunlight streaming outward in all directions. From each of these beams of glorious light healing flows."[1]

Curses

Scripture refers to sins that are passed down from generation to generation. They can affect the entire family—even children in the third and fourth generations of those who reject God (Exod. 20:5). We often defend ourselves with, "It just runs in my family. I can't help my temper because my mother had a bad temper." Such statements are used to justify any number of other undesirable behaviors. Some of the problems arise from the fact that we observed firsthand these traits in our family environment as they were modeled in front of us. In addition, they may be passed down as part of our spiritual DNA. Just as we have a physical DNA that determines our eye color, hair, size, and other features, so we have an inheritance of character traits. It is wonderful to have the godly positive traits passed down, but it is not so wonderful to find ourselves in possession of ungodly, undesirable traits.

Freedom from these curses was provided at the cross, but the children of God must know this and claim it for themselves. We have become part of a royal family with the perfect blood of Jesus as provision for our defects. His blood atoned for our freedom from the curses passed down through our family bloodlines. These curses are chains that bind us until we assert our God-given authority and command them to be removed from us in the name of Jesus and through his blood provision.

Eyes to See

It is helpful to read about the life of Jesus as recorded in the Bible in the gospels of Matthew, Mark, Luke, and John. Many of the same stories are repeated in each book. Scripture relates Jesus saying, "The Father and I are one" (John 10:30 NLT). The way Jesus interacted with people shows the nature of God in that Jesus was gentle, patient, and kind. Nevertheless, he did not gloss over sin. He told the woman caught in adultery to "Go and sin no more" (John 8:11 NLT). The life of Jesus should be our guide for living and our guide for the treatment of others. Identify and feel his compassion as he reaches out with the hope of a new life to a lost, dying, sinful, and hurting humanity.

Obedience

If we choose to obey Scripture and live out its principles, even when we are just beginning with baby steps, we demonstrate our sincere obedience to God. He comes and provides the power we need as we step out and yield our self-interest, self-protection, and self-assertion. In fact, he will do it for us—our job is to surrender the ever-present and insistent self-life to him. The indwelling Holy Spirit is more than desirous of flowing through us to a world in need of witnessing his presence and power. This is made possible as we allow him control of our feelings, actions, and reactions.

As we determine not to be offended and not to hold onto unforgiveness, then more of God's light shines through us to the world around us. We discover our own uniqueness! We are better able to find our true identity. It is no longer covered up by others' opinions, labels, or expectations.

We have looked at ways to control our thoughts, and how to speak faith-filled words over our lives and situations. Guidelines for healthy friendships have been explored. We discussed the great freedom to be found as we surrender to God all of the situations of our lives. Having determined to live our lives by these principles, we can come to the Father in prayer and fellowship with no shame and no barriers! We learn not to struggle in his ways and presence, but rather to snuggle down in the green meadows he has provided.

The Good Shepherd

Consider the concept of God as the Good Shepherd and that we are his sheep. This picture will help us understand some additional principles that will help us break free and to stay free of the chains that have held us captive.

Rest/Water/Food

Early in the day dew lies on grass in the pasture. The sheep can be refreshed as they lie down to rest in the cool blades. We can also be rejuvenated as we come early in the day for rest in the presence of the Good Shepherd. This is rest for our spirits, but it also manifests in rest for our bodies as the spirit and the physical influence each other greatly.

As we commune with God, we should tell him our needs, desires, and problems. If we do this we can let go of the burdens we are carrying and experience peace.

The story is told of a traveler who held his heavy baggage throughout a long train trip. Upon arrival at his destination someone asked, "Why didn't you put your baggage down?" "I didn't know there was a place I could put it down," he replied. It is a relief to know that Jesus has provided a place for us to put our baggage. He wants our burdens, whether heavy, oppressive, or simply perplexing. "Give your burdens to the LORD, and he will take care of you. He will not permit the godly to slip and fall" (Ps. 55:22 NLT).

Grace had to struggle as she learned to put a burden down. She had to put aside her own agenda and dreams for her daughter, who gave birth to a biracial baby out of wedlock. The daughter continued college and after graduation got back together with Jack, the father of the baby. Grace and her husband, as well as her extended family, put their prejudices aside. Grace's father, who was the most prejudiced, shook the young man's hand the first time they met and told him he was always welcome.

Grace and her husband opened their hearts and minds; they welcomed Jack and loved him. Two years after the birth of the child Grace saw Jack come to faith in Jesus and be baptized. Subsequently, the couple was married at a small chapel with family and had a wonderful reception at a beautiful cabin in the mountains of Tennessee. They now have their daughter in a Christian preschool where she is learning Christian principles. Grace said, "I am in *awe* of God and ask him to forgive me my unbelief. He worked out the difficult situation better than I could ever think or imagine."

Scripture speaks of the Word of God as water for cleansing our spirits (Eph. 5:26). Our parched lives are watered as we read, speak, and study the Word of God. Sheep graze on grass for food. Our spiritual food is the Word of God, which feeds our faith. In his letter to the Romans, Paul said, "Consequently, faith comes from hearing the message, and the message is heard through the word of Christ" (10:17 NIV). The Bible provides nourishment for our emotional well-being. As our spirits are fed it spills over and affects our physical well-being.

Healthy sheep graze often. Likewise we must consult the Word on a daily basis so that our spirits are fed.

SAFETY

The sheep are safe in the pasture under the shepherd's watchful eye. He will see danger and avert it, or he will show the sheep the right path to take around or through it. The shepherd has a rod by which he guides the straying sheep back to the fold. Just so for us, safety is found as we stay in the pasture (God's best for our life) and not try to wander away from the safety provided by the shepherd. The sheep that stray may encounter enemies ready to strike them down. In addition, there may be dangerous terrain in an unfamiliar part of the pasture.

Staying Free

We have explored a number of areas to rid ourselves of the chains that bind in order for us to become free men and women. How do we stay free? Here are some keys:

Key 1 is Obedience

Obedience is a big key. Without obedience the blessings of the Father for his children are blocked. Picture a pipe through which blessings flow down from heaven to us here on earth. If that pipe is clogged up with issues of offense, hatred, unforgiveness, and resentment, then God's blessings are crowded out. Just as sheep know the voice of the shepherd, so we learn to recognize the inner promptings and thoughts that come to us from Jesus, our good Shepherd. In addition to this we have many clear instructions and guidelines offered in Scripture to determine what our behavior should be.

Key 2 is Praise

"Praise lifts our eyes from our circumstances to our Almighty Father who is ruler over all. Praise lifts your eyes from the battle to the victory, for Christ is already victor, and though we do not yet see all things under His feet, they are there (Heb. 2:8, Eph. 1:22) in the realm of the Spirit. Praise will sweeten and hallow all that it touches. Praise will kindle a new faith. Praise will fan the sparks of your smoldering love into a flaming love for God."[2]

It has been stated previously that praise does not come naturally to some of us. We can learn to have a thankful heart and be lifted into a spirit of praise by reading the Old Testament book of Psalms in the Bible. It is especially helpful to read them aloud. It has also been stated that remembering the faithfulness of God in previous situations serves as a great motivation for praise.

KEY 3 IS PRAYER

It is an awesome thought to know that the God of the universe desires and waits to hear from each of his children. He is available for those who will make the time to quiet themselves in his presence. Of course, he is also there in daily situations, as we call on him for help in emergencies. He is there as well for things that come up unexpectedly when we need wisdom to know how to proceed.

It is best not to approach God in prayer with an outstretched hand that is completely need-oriented. Rather, first come to God with hands stretched out like a child reaching for its parent. We can learn to experience the beautiful pleasures to be found as we sit quietly and nurture an atmosphere where we can receive his love for our parched, thirsty, love-hungry souls.

KEY 4 IS THE NAME

Jesus is the name above every name. All power was given by God the Father to Jesus. Scripture says, "That power is like the working of his mighty strength, which he exerted in Christ when he raised him from the dead and seated him at his right hand in the heavenly realms, far above all rule and authority, power and dominion, and every title that can be given, not only in the present age but also in the one to come. And God placed all things under his feet and appointed him to be head over everything for the church" (Eph. 1:19–22 NIV). Since all power is given to Jesus, Scripture tells us to ask in the name of Jesus: "And I will do whatever you ask in my name, so that the Son may bring glory to the Father" (John 14:13 NIV). "And give thanks for everything to God the Father in the name of our Lord Jesus Christ" (Eph. 5:20 NLT). We are privileged to be able to pray in the name that represents all of the power of the Godhead. His name is the authority through which we make our petitions.

KEY 5 IS THE BLOOD OF JESUS

"For the life of a creature is in the blood, and I have given it to you to make atonement for yourselves on the altar; it is the blood that makes atonement for one's life" (Lev. 17:11 NIV). All life is in the blood; the life of Jesus is in the blood. When we, by faith, call on the power of the blood of Christ, we are calling for the life of Jesus to come to bear on the situation facing us.[3]

"When we point to the blood sacrifice provided by Jesus Christ at the cross, we are calling on the power of his life to come to bear on the situations we face. Each time we proclaim, in faith, the power of the blood, we are bringing the life force of Jesus Christ to bear upon whatever crisis is at hand. We claim and proclaim the blood of Jesus and command Satan to loose his grip in the name of Jesus. We always remember that it is the indwelling Holy Spirit who gives us strength to do this."[4]

Walking Free

"It is through Him that we enjoy a magnificent inner security and through Him that we go out to engage in an adventurous life of new-found freedom under His direction."[5] The pathway to freedom beckons each of us to come and walk as free men and women. The chains will fall off. You will experience freedom. "If the Son sets you free, you are truly free" (John 8:36 NLT).

Walk Free! Will you make this life changing choice?

ENDNOTES

Chapter 2: Discover Your True Identity

1. Marie Chapian, *Mothers and Daughters* (Minneapolis, MN: Bethany House, 1988), 63.
2. Ibid., 118.
3. Calvin Miller, *The Power in Letting Go* (Wheaton, IL: Tyndale House, 2003), 79.

Chapter 3: Freedom from Tormenting Thoughts

1. Tommy Newberry, *The 4:8 Principle* (Carol Stream, IL: Tyndale House), xvii.
2. Frances P. Martin, *Hung by the Tongue* (Lafayette, LA: F.P.M. Publications, 1979), 18.

Chapter 4: Chains of Offense

1. Frances Frangipane, "Unoffendable," www.frangipane.org web archives, June 22, 2007.
2. Ibid.

Chapter 5: Free to Forgive

1. Jack W. Hayford, *Why can't We All Get Along?* Message paper, 2005. Mailed to supporters.
2. David Wilkerson, *The Power of Forgiveness*, Pulpit Paper, July 25, 2005. Mailed to supporters.
3. Ibid.
4. R.T. Kendall, *Total Forgiveness* (Lake Mary, FL: Charisma House, 2002), 182.
5. Grant Mullen, Teaching C.D. *A Physician's View of Healing* (Burlington, Ontario, Canada Orchard View Medical Media), www.drgrantmullen.com.

Chapter 6: The Power of Words

1. John F. Stephens in Francis P. Martin, *Hung by the Tongue* (Lafayette, LA: F. P. M. Publications, 1979), Foreword.
2. E.W. Kenyon, *The Power of Your Words* (New Kensington, PA: Whitaker House, 1981), 9.
3. Ibid., 27.
4. Ibid., 21.
5. Martin, 28.

Chapter 8: Surrender the Burden

1. Calvin Miller, *The Power in Letting Go* (Wheaton, IL: Tyndale House, 2003), 23.
2. Stavate Silouan, *The Undistorted Image* Archimandrite Publisher translated by Rosemary Edmonds (Sofrony 1958), 157.
3. Carol Kent, *When I Lay My Isaac Down* (Colorado Springs, CO, Navpress Publishing, 2004), 33.
4. Ibid., 53.
5. Miller, ix.

Chapter 9: No Shame, No Chains, Free to Know God

1. *New Spirit-Filled Bible NKJV* (Nashville, TN: Thomas Nelson, 2004), note 1273.

2. *Praise is Faith at Work*, Pamphlet (Minneapolis, MN: Osterhus Publishing House).
3. Peggy Park, *The Power of the Lamb's Blood* (Enumclaw, WA: WinePress, 2004), P. 93.
4. Ibid., 95–96.
5. Phillip Keller, *A Shepherd Looks at the Good Shepherd and His Sheep* (Grand Rapids, MI: Zondervan, 1978), 88–89.